The

Q....l.l.

compiled by
Al Dixon

Hill Street Press **d** Athens, Georgia

A HILL STREET PRESS BOOK

Published in the United States of America by Hill Street Press LLC
191 East Broad Street, Suite 209 ➨ Athens, Georgia 30601-2848 USA
706-613-7200 ➨ info@hillstreetpress.com ➨ www.hillstreetpress.com

Hill Street Press gratefully acknowledges the generosity of the *Oxford American* in whose pages many of these quotations first appeared. For more information about "the Southern magazine of good writing," please visit www.oxfordamericanmag.com. ➨ Hill Street Press books are available in bulk purchase and customized editions to institutions and corporate accounts. Please contact us for more information. ➨ No material in this book may be reproduced, scanned, stored, or transmitted in any form, including all electronic and print media, or otherwise used without the prior written consent of the publisher. However, an excerpt not to exceed 500 words may be used one time only by newspaper and magazine editors solely in conjunction with a review of or feature article about this book, the author, or Hill Street Press, LLC. Attribution must be provided including the publisher's name, author's name, and title of the book.

Library of Congress Cataloging-in-Publication Data

The quotable South / edited by Al Dixon.
     p.   cm.
   ISBN 1-58818-090-5
   1. Southern State—Quotations, maxims, etc. I. Dixon, Al, 1971–
PN6084.S7 Q68 2001   2001024052
975—dc21

ISBN # 1-58818-090-5

10 9 8 7 6 5 4 3 2 1

First printing

Foreword

A Southern quotation will make you stop and think.

I say that, but come to think of it—

Stop doing what? Weren't you thinking already? What were you doing, just moseying along? Or maybe eating something so good it rendered ratiocination moot?

And all of a sudden here come a Southern quotation up the road tipping its hat and saying "Hidy, Br'er Reader," and *then* you started to think?

Too late. In a sense, a Southern quotation is like a chigger bite: once it begins to sink in, you're going to have to live with it awhile. Your only chance of dealing with a Southern quotation is to see it coming. Even if you're drinking, can't you be thinking—sort of—at the same time? Consider the Larry Brown quotation in this book:

> I had some beer iced down in the truck. They got a crazy law in this county. You can't go into a store and buy cold beer; you can only buy it hot. So you . . . have to always be thinking ahead.

Okay. Say you are *ready* for a Southern quotation. Now. Are you willing to go along with it? Bear in mind that a Southern quotation is liable to say almost anything. One minute a Southern quotation will be saying you can tell a Southerner by the knife-fight scars. The next minute, by the thank-you notes. If it's the only way to get at something, a Southern quotation will even shade the truth.

But you say to me, "What if I feel, within myself, what could be a Southern quotation *coming on?*"

That's different. Your best policy there is that of the Reverend Sam Jones, as quoted herein: "When I get up to preach, all I do is to knock out the bung and let nature cut her caper."

ROY BLOUNT JR.

A Few Words of
Wisdom

If you fear making anyone mad, then you probe
for the lowest common denominator of human
achievement.

Jimmy Carter

Boy, don't you know better than to crap
under your tree?

Tony Earley's father to Earley,
after he committed the cardinal sin of deer hunters

I cut the nuts off hogs. I dig screwworms out of a cow.
And the cow is lowing and screaming and frothing at the
mouth, but that's all right, you just dig 'em out and put the
tar in, and hope she lives.

Harry Crews

Nobody with a good car needs to be justified.

Hazel Motes, in Flannery O'Connor's "Wise Blood"

What I found to be important is mainly just the realization
that everyone has all knowledge and all humanity within
themselves. Individual minds are connected to a universal
mind. All people need to do is find out how to get it and
reach it when they need it. Karma is simple truth: you reap
what you sow.

Willie Nelson

~~~~~~

We can either be lonely or Alone.

Jean Toomer, Essentials

~~~~

Everybody please take my advice, I ain't gonna tell you
    nothin' wrong,
Everybody please take my advice, I ain't gonna tell you
    nothin' wrong.
Boy, don't let whiskey and them women make you break up
    your happy home.

Big Bill Broonzy, "Advice Blues"

~~~~

Follow your instincts. That's where true
wisdom manifests itself.

Oprah Winfrey

~~~~

**The way I see it, if you want the rainbow, you
gotta put up with the rain.**

Dolly Parton

~~~~~~

Between grief and nothing, I will take grief.

William Faulkner, The Wild Palms

Life's under no obligation to give us what we expect. We take what we get and are thankful it's no worse than it is.

Margaret Mitchell

It's a lot better to be seen than heard. The sun is the most powerful thing I know of, and it doesn't make much noise.

Bear Bryant

Courage is contagious. When a brave man takes a stand, the spines of others are stiffened.

Billy Graham

Daddy always says if you give a man a white shirt and a tie and a suit of clothes, you can find out real quick how sorry he is.

Harry Crews

Win if you can, lose if you must, always cheat, and if they take you out, leave tearing down the ring.

Motto of 1950s Memphis wrestler Sputnik Monroe

A fair amount of what's wrong with the world on any particular day . . . is apt to be somebody's unwillingness to experience something he's never experienced before.

Steve Yarbrough

It's a sin to kill a mockingbird.

Atticus Finch, in Harper Lee's To Kill a Mockingbird

All her life my mother told me, "No matter how poor you are, you can always be clean."

Andrew Hudgins

If you're bored with your life, risk it.

James Dickey

A mule can climb a tree if it's in love.

Barry Hannah

One for the cutworm, one for the crow, one to rot, and one to grow.

Old rule for planting corn

What is the South?

south *n* **1**: the direction to the right of one facing east **2** :
the compass point directly opposite to north **3** *cap*: regions
or countries south of a specified or implied point; *esp*: the
southeastern part of the U.S.

> The Merriam-Webster Dictionary

There are two ways of looking at the South.
What is it? And *Who* is it? . . . I prefer the second
question, for the South is the people who live
there.

> *Albert Gore Sr.*, Let the Glory Out

Not exactly a nation within a nation but the closest thing to it.

W. J. Cash's description of the South

Over the past century and a half, what is considered "The South" has slid down the Atlantic seaboard. Maryland and Delaware no longer belong to it, and even northern Virginia is suspect.

Fred Hobson

The South is the only place in the world where nothing has to be explained to me.

Woodrow Wilson

The South. The poor South.

John C. Calhoun's last words

I suggest that the true Southland is that territory within which, when asked by an outsider whether he is a Southerner, the reply almost invariably is "Hell, yes!"

Hamilton Horton

The South—where roots, place, family, and tradition are the essence of identity.

Social historian Carl N. Degler

The South is America. The South is what we started out with in this bizarre, slightly troubling, basically wonderful country—fun, danger, friendliness, energy, enthusiasm, and brave, crazy, tough people.

P. J. O'Rourke

Alabama, for some reason I cannot determine, seems to me to be the most Southern state of the South.

Pearl Buck

Florida has its own North and South, but its northern area is strictly Southern, and its Southern area definitely Northern.

Florida: A Guide to the Southernmost State

The South always makes good reading. It features the virtues and vices, writ large, of the nation as a whole. It's good entertainment. It's high drama.

Fred Hobson

The South was always a schizophrenic place, of two minds about everything.

John Egerton

The thing, I have to say, that I love about the South: it tends to cherish and elevate its eccentrics, rather than try to do a psychiatric diagnosis of why they are the way they are.

Floyd Carlisle, composer of the operas Susannah, Willie Stark, *and* Cold Sassy Tree

Of the making of books about the South there is no end.

Clyde N. Wilson

But there's something about the Southland in the springtime
Where the water flows with confidence and reason.
When God made me born a Yankee he was teasin'.
There's no place like home and none more pleasin'
Than the Southland in the springtime.

Indigo Girls, "Southland in the Springtime"

What has always been clear, for Southerner and non-Southerner alike, is that Dixie is the most fascinating part of the country. There may be a book out there called *The Great Midwest* or *A Turn in the Midwest* or *The Mind of the Midwest* or *The Midwestern Mystique*, but if there is I'm certainly not aware of it.

Fred Hobson

The South has had its full share of illusions, fantasies, and pretensions, and it has continued to cling to some of them with an astonishing tenacity that defies explanation.

C. Vann Woodward

What Is a Southerner?

What could be more Southern than to obsess about being Southern?

Elizabeth Fortson Arroyo

~~~

I go back to the South, physically and in my memories, to remind myself who I am, for the South keeps me going.

Willie Morris

~~~

What I came to know about Willie Morris was that an innate and profound Southernness was the energizing force in his life.

William Styron

Country folks'll get their wives to whack their hair off with a knife before they'll pay that price.

Ernest Oliver, a barber in Oxford, Mississippi, since 1942, reacting when told that some people in New York will pay forty dollars for a haircut

My sister says Southerners are like other people, only more so.

Blanche McCrary Boyd

Everything about me that is still Southern is something that I have held on to because it is tasty.

Roy Blount Jr.

Because we have a president who is from Arkansas, I now confess that I, too, am from Arkansas, and not from Shanghai or Sewickley, Pennsylvania, as I used to claim.

John Fergus Ryan

Southern Comfort. How can that be, I wonder?

Blanche Dubois, in Tennessee Williams's A Streetcar Named Desire

**I wouldn't be a lawyer a-pleading at the bar;
I'd rather be a soldier and wear the Southern star.
I wouldn't be a doctor a-waiting on the sick;
I'd rather be a soldier and go in double quick.**

Confederate ballad

Southerners can never resist a losing cause.

Margaret Mitchell

Down South everybody cherishes dreams. In dreams this world and the next mix like sugar and grits.

Grandmother Ernestine, to novelist Jewell Parker Rhodes

Life is like a box of chocolates, Forrest. You never know what you're gonna get.

Winston Groom, Forrest Gump

Southerners all like to generalize. That is the only way in this world you are ever going to get down to universal truth.

Roy Blount Jr.

The Southerner is often inspired to do his best when the odds are heaviest against him, when he knows it, when he knows further that the world knows it and is looking on.

Thomas Wolfe

I am a Southerner and an American.

Jimmy Carter

~~~~

We Southerners are a mythological people, created half out of dream and half out of slander.

Jonathan Daniels

~~~~

Southerners seem more likely than other Americans to think of their region . . . possessively as theirs.

John Shelton Reed

~~~~

I haven't been this happy in a long time. It's the sensual texture of things here. It's the wood smoke that's in the air on a dreary winter day. It's the chicken and barbecue that they sell in little stores and service stations. It's the conversations about people from the past with old family names that intertwine.

Willie Morris, on returning to the South

We love the South with a fierce, protective
passion such as parents have for a crippled child.

Ralph McGill

Boy, but the barbecue is still fine and the air is still clean
and you can drive along in a car and tell what who is having
for dinner.

*Ralph Ellison, on returning to his home town
of Oklahoma City*

Because I was born in the South, I'm a
Southerner. If I had been born in the North,
the West, or the Central Plains, I would be a
human being.

Clyde Edgerton

When a New Yorker asked a Savannah society woman what she did, she looked at him, puzzled. "Why, ah *live*—ah *live* in Sa-vannah!" she replied with proper hauteur.

> *Rosemary Daniell,* Sleeping with Soldiers:
> In Search of the Macho Man

The Southerner has always tended to believe with his blood rather than his intellect.

> *Marshall Frady*

I don't think of myself as a Negro. I'm a Southerner. I just like the Southern way of life.

> *Julian Bond*

Southerners are generally polite and unpretentious; perhaps it's too hot to be otherwise.

> *Blanche McCrary Boyd*

It is important for me to be a Southerner, for a
Jew to be a Jew, or whatever else a man might be.

James Dickey

In the South our anxiety is not to find new ideas, but to bring
to realization old ones which have been tested and proved by
years of anguish—a far more difficult undertaking.

William Alexander Percy

Attempts at self-interpretation have
become one of [the South's] most
characteristic cultural products.

Drew Gilpin Faust

Kin

Southerners can claim kin with anybody. It's one of our most dextrous talents.

Guy Davenport

To this day Southerners acknowledge a more far-flung kin network . . . than people in other regions of the United States.

Social historian Carl N. Degler

It doesn't matter where in the South you go, because the entire South seems to be married to one another.

Marilyn Schwartz

By 1800, any given individual was likely to be a
cousin, in one degree or another, to practically
everybody within a radius of thirty miles about him.
And his circle of kin, of course, overlapped more or
less with the next, and that in turn with the next
beyond, and so on in an endless web, through the
whole South.

W. J. Cash

You Would Have To Be
Born There

You can't understand it. You would have to be born there.

> *Quentin Compson (referring to the South) to Shreve, in William Faulkner's* Absalom, Absalom!

The South, to Yankees and Other Foreigners

"No, no, no," her magazine editors were always saying to her. "Give us the real Mississippi, little old black men playing harmonicas, and roosters in barnyards, and rednecks, and Confederate flags. That's what we want. Give us the real squalor."

> *Cynthia Shearer, "Still Life with Shotgun and Oranges"*

A New York friend said that visiting the South reminded her of nothing more than being in high school again.

Rosemary Daniell

Even today the Northern visitor hankers to see eroded hills and rednecks, scrub cotton and sharecropper shacks.

John T. Westbrook

A volitionless, almost helpless capacity to believe anything about the South not even provided it be derogatory but merely bizarre enough and strange enough.

Gavin Stephens, describing the gullibility of Northeners, in William Faulkner's Intruder in the Dust

It's better than Ben Hur.

Shreve to Quentin, discussing the South, in William Faulker's Absalom, Absalom!

Our hills are the most isolated area of America, the subject of countless doctoral theses. It's an odd sensation to read about yourself as counterpart to the aborigine or Eskimo.

> *Kentucky-born Chris Offutt,*
> *"The Same River Twice: A Memoir"*

Maybe Northern people just ask me about the abundance of Southern writers so that I will feel better about being from the South.

> *Roy Blount Jr.*

By necessity, I think most Southerners subscribe to Keats's concept of negative capability in which "man is capable of being in uncertainties, Mysteries, doubts, without any irritable reaching after fact and reason." Yankees have a harder time with this.

> *Julia Reed*

Oh, Alabama.
The Devil fools with the best-laid plans.

> *Neil Young, "Alabama"*

Don't think that you know what's
going on.

*John Shelton Reed, "Rules for Successful Adjustment
to the South"*

**It was not very much the café society he was
used to living in.**

*Mary Gay Shipley, owner of a bookstore in Blytheville,
Arkansas, speaking about Ernest Hemingway's visits to his
second wife's hometown in rural Arkansas*

The farce of the vulgar rich has its foundations in
Mississippi, as in New York and Manchester, in the
rapidity with which certain values have advanced, especially
that of cotton, and simultaneously, that of cotton land and
Negroes.

Frederick Law Olmsted

Northerners, provincials that they are, regard the South as one large Mississippi. Southerners, with their eye for distinction, place Mississippi in a class by itself.

V. O. Key Jr.

Take it all in all, our sojourn in Savannah was pleasant, far better than we expected, and my recollections of it are of an agreeable nature. Many a time afterward, I regretted leaving it.

Union Army officer J. Madison Drake, in his 1880 memoir of his company's internment during the Civil War, Fast and Loose in Dixie

My goal in life is to make some tiny headway toward lifting from Southerners some tiny bit of the burden of having to prove [to Northerners] that we are being tongue-in-cheek.

Roy Blount Jr.

A foreigner from Scotland or California visits a large Southern city—usually Atlanta—and complains that he could never find the South of song and story. Just another Minneapolis, as far as he could see, with the heat turned up and a few magnolias.

Hal Crowther

You're wearing a suit. I thought you'd be chewing on a blade of grass.

A woman in Manhattan, on meeting Roy Blount Jr.

Double-wide what?

A note Lee Smith's New York copy editor wrote in the margin of one of her manuscripts

I definitely want to relocate. Somewhere in the South. . . . I just wanna be able to relax.

The Notorious B.I.G., in an interview shortly before his death

In the back seat was a short story writer from Iowa who, until I took him to one, had never seen a cotton field and who, until I enticed him to, had never danced on a table. Don't worry—I said to him as we boogied—it's only Mississippi, you'll be fine when you get home.

Beverly Lowry

I had an interesting experience at Rutgers University, where one of these classic Northeastern liberals on the faculty there—someone who came of age in the sixties and who was so interested and involved in civil rights that Mississippi for him was the personification of evil—absolutely refused to hear that Mississippi could have been anything other than evil in the forties and fifties.

John Howard, on criticism of his book Men Like That: A Southern Queer History

YOU
WOULD
HAVE
TO
BE
BORN
THERE

To His Excellency President LINCOLN, *Washington, D.C.:*

I beg to present you as a Christmas-gift the city of Savannah, with one hundred and fifty heavy guns and plenty of ammunition, also about twenty-five thousand bales of cotton.

> *W. T. SHERMAN, Major-General.*
>
> *Telegram to Lincoln from Sherman on December 22, 1864, after invading the city*

With all the faults of the South, I love her still.

> *Abolitionist Emily Pillsbury Burke,* Pleasure and Pain: Reminiscences of Georgia in the 1840s

Southerners Abroad

The South has changed rapidly, but it doesn't take many trips to New York to persuade you that its image has not.

> *Hal Crowther*

If I'm performing at a county fair in upstate New York, and I say "Me and Marcel Ledbetter went coon huntin'," . . . I explain coon huntin'. If I'm in Alabama, I just say, "We went coon huntin'," and go right on with the story.

> *Jerry Clower*

I think if I'd stayed in the South, I might have been anti-Southern, but I became a Southerner again by going East.

> *Allen Tate*

In Mississippi, or in Texas, "friends" had been people whom one saw frequently and informally. . . . [In New York] one could call a person a "friend" if you saw him once every four or five months, talked for a while, and got along.

> *Willie Morris*

YOU
WOULD
HAVE
TO
BE
BORN
THERE

If it's easy to be a native of Birmingham
when you live in Atlanta, it's even easier
when you live in northern Illinois.

Alan Jacobs

**Our aim in life during those days was to go to
New York and often we would just look at the
parked cars with New York license plates and
dream about the time when we, too, could go to
the magic city.**

Carson McCullers

He felt more at home with Southerners, with whom he
could share tall tales and indigenous jokes and family
anecdotes and hilarious yarns that only the South can
provide, and that perhaps only expatriate Southerners can
enjoy in their cloying and sometimes desperate
homesickness.

William Styron, remembering writer and editor Willie Morris

There's a wonderful sense of graciousness and kindness in the South that you don't have anywhere else. Plus, we have a terrible time trying to find good pork barbeque in New York.

Memphis native Kenneth Jackson, chair of the history department at Columbia University

Take me home. I was born in the South; I have lived and labored in the South; and I wish to die and be buried in the South.

Booker T. Washington

All Southerners go home sooner or later, even if in a box.

Truman Capote

Deep down I knew I could never really leave the South, for my feelings had already been formed by the South.

Richard Wright

Now I live in New York and Massachusetts, but that is because when I'm in the South I wander around wondering where I can get *The New York Times,* and when I'm in the North I wander around wondering where I can get some okra, and I would rather think about some okra than *The New York Times.*

Roy Blount Jr.

I never knew I was Southern until I moved to Laramie, Wyoming, in 1980. . . . Up until then I mistook myself for a citizen of the world— you know, with an accent.

Nanci Kincaid

The South on Screen and Stage

Hollywood has always had a patronizing attitude toward the South. I couldn't sit through *Gone with the Wind*, it was so bad. There should be a line of guys with shotguns at the Mason-Dixon Line to tell actors, "You can't come here unless you know what you're doing."

> *Robert Duvall*

People in this country do not think that evil Southerners are cool. Our bad guys are not ready for cable.

> *Roy Blount Jr.*

Most of the time he sounds like Strom Thurmond with a bad cold and a mouth full of mashed potatoes.

> *Randall Curb, on Orson Welles's performance as a*
> *Southerner in* The Long, Hot Summer

Had I been more alert, it might have occurred to me that somehow a group of white Alabama farm folk had learned of my presence in New York, thrown together a theatrical troupe, and flown north to haunt me.

Ralph Ellison, on first seeing the Broadway production of Tobacco Road *in New York*

I wanted to free his plays from the kitchen-sink realism, the pretty quality, that had trapped his works since the 1950s.

Robert Falls, on directing plays by Tennessee Williams

The essence of drama is change, and the section of the country that is most in flux appears to be the South; therefore, I go there to make films.

Martin Ritt, director of The Long, Hot Summer *and* The Sound and the Fury, *based on works by William Faulkner*

All [Oliver Stone's] editing frenzy can't save Kevin Costner from a tepid persona or that accent.

Randy Thornton, on Costner's performance in JFK

When the Southern Cinema Hall of Fame is finally dedicated, there'll be a sanctified Robert Mitchum Wing.

Randy Thornton

When a small town in the South dresses its young ladies for a beauty pageant or centennial celebration, its model is England's Vivien Leigh in *Gone with the Wind* **or New England's Bette Davis in** *Jezebel.*

Hal Crowther

For the entire state of Georgia, having the premiere of *Gone With the Wind* on home ground was like winning the Battle of Atlanta seventy-five years late.

Anne Edwards

YOU
WOULD
HAVE
TO
BE
BORN
THERE

Them's Fightin' Words

For all its size and wealth and all the "progress" it babbles of, [the South] is almost as sterile, artistically, intellectually, culturally, as the Sahara Desert.

> *H. L. Mencken*

~~~

This is like the thief who robs the house the second time and complains that the owners do not eat with silver.

> *Andrew Lytle, responding to H. L. Mencken's dismissal of the South as "the Sahara of the Bozart"*

As a general statement, I don't like Yankees. I'm as polite as I can be, but I don't like their behavior. I've had occasions to tell some Yankees that they wouldn't stay alive two days in the counties I come from, acting the way they act, talking the way they talk, shoving people out of the way. You can't do that.

Harry Crews

You can spot them by their yards, which they don't care too much about. . . . They hang out a sign on the front of their trailer that says "Hans and Frieda," and then they go inside and play cards the rest of their lives.

Description of Yankees, in Nanci Kincaid's "Crossing Blood"

If you are going to be underestimated by people who speak more rapidly, the temptation is to speak slowly and strategically and outwit them.

Doris Betts, on the Southern drawl

Can they hit Oxford, Mississippi?

Robert F. Kennedy, on hearing that Soviet weapons had been discovered in Cuba three weeks after the riots against the integration of Ole Miss

Southern man, better keep your head.
Don't forget what your good book said.

Neil Young, "Southern Man"

Well I hope Neil Young will remember A Southern man don't need him around anyhow.

Lynyrd Skynard, "Sweet Home, Alabama"

Since there's no route to national recognition that doesn't run through New York, Southern writers are obliged to grit their teeth and steer a course somewhere between hysterical Yankee-bashing and mute despair.

Hal Crowther

The deep-dyed fear that lives in the heart of every Southerner, myself included, [is] that a Yankee is putting us down.

Julia Reed

~~~

You in the North always assume there are two attitudes toward the race question—one pre-empted by the enlightened benign citizens of Northern birth, the other peculiar to the narrow heartless citizen of Southern birth. There is no such difference.

William Alexander Percy

~~~

Beyond the mountains was the North: the land of Damyankess, where live People Who Cause Us All of Our Trouble

Lillian Smith

41
THEM'S
FIGHTIN'
WORDS

Fundamentalism, Ku Kluxry, revivals, lynchings, hog wallow politics—these are the things that always occur to a Northerner when he thinks of the South.

H. L. Mencken

Dave Gardner never got around to organizing his National Association for the Advancement of White Trash, so it's still okay to portray Southern whites as amusing nincompoops.

John Shelton Reed

As long as popular culture persists in presenting them as incestuous hillbillies, church-burners, mule-beaters, and randy evangelists, Southerners will dip snuff and fly Confederate battle flags just to make New Yorkers wince.

Hal Crowther

Southerners are probably not more hospitable than New Englanders are; they are simply more willing to remind you of the fact they are being hospitable.

Ray L. Birdwhistle

Yeah, Mississippi. They say it's last in everything. They ain't telling me anything. I know it's last.

Rockabilly legend Charlie Feathers

The horses and the numbers keep most of them alive. All they eat is hot dogs when eatin' time arrives.

Margaret Johnson, "Folks in New York City Ain't Like the Folks Back South"

The North isn't a place. It's just a direction out of the South.

Roy Blount Jr.

Ohio! Ohio! Imp of Satan, don't you know where Ohio is?

> *Aunt Irene, in Walter Sullivan's* The Long, Long Love, *in response to his question, "What would I be doing if I had been born in Ohio rather than in Tennessee?"*

I think there's hope in the South, not in the North.

Alice Walker

Clean up the South: Buy a Yankee a bus ticket.

A bumper sticker

The only good thing that ever came out of Chicago was I-65 South.

Lewis Grizzard

The Southern Woman

What Southern women are is loyal, very sexy, polite to a
fault, and when necessary, razor-sharp in their wit. And
most importantly, a Southern woman (when pushed) will—
in every possible meaning of the phrase—"Kick your ass!"

Branford Marsalis

Women on Women

More than anything, more than they are obsessed with
appearances, more than they like to look soft or ladylike,
more than they like to stop a room or win a man or an
argument or a seat at the table with what they are wearing,
Southern women know how to rise to the occasion.

Julia Reed

The only thing that separates us from the animals is our ability to accessorize.

Clairee Belcher, in Robert Harling's Steel Magnolias

Nobody can be exactly like me. Sometimes even I have trouble doing it.

Tallulah Bankhead

The biggest myth about Southern women is that we are frail, neurasthenic types, fainting on our sofas behind closed doors. . . . Nobody in the Appalachian South where I grew up (no columns, no money, no landed aristocracy— hell, no land!) ever acted like that. We were about as fragile as coal trucks.

Lee Smith

Many Southern Ladies are fierce, dignified ex-Belles who changed their ways before they went crazy or killed somebody.

Donna Tartt

Southern women are the only women who still have the glamour of days gone by. That's why we're so high maintenance.

> *Female impersonator Lady Chablis, of* Midnight in the Garden of Good and Evil *fame*

A lot of times, a Southern woman is so capable, and so used to having to do things for herself anyway, that she fails to notice that the guy hasn't met her challenge. This is the reason that most of my friends who got married are now divorced.

> *Julia Reed*

In general, [historians] agree that the function of Southern womanhood has been to justify the perpetuation of the hegemony of the male sex, the upper and middle classes, and the white race.

> *Anne Goodwyn Jones, in* The Encyclopedia of Southern Culture

Southern ladies like to be gracious. Above all, they love to entertain. They love to make their home an inviting place and then invite people into it, make them feel comfortable, surrounded by lovely things, and feasting on delicious foods.

Phyllis Hoffman, founder of Southern Lady *magazine*

Down South my folks felt eight grades of schooling was enough. After all, I was already pledged to be a clerk's wife. I knew how to cook and clean. I served in the church, passing out fans with portraits of Jesus to folks who cried and shivered with the Holy Spirit.

Grandmother Ernestine, to novelist Jewell Parker Rhodes

It's the good girls who keep the diaries; the bad girls never have the time.

Tallulah Bankhead

Don't tell me I can't do something, cause I'll show you I can.

Tammy Wynette to her first husband, who scoffed at her dream to be a country music star

She was so huge and soft it was like embracing a cloud and sinking down into it; she smelt of liquor, nicotine, and cheap perfume and powder—loose powder, the kind one finds for sale in dime stores.

Lee Smith, Oral History

I have always said that next to Imperial China, the South is the best place in the world to be an old lady.

Florence King

Some of us bad girls grew up in rough neighborhoods, where you just hit them back. Victim mentality hadn't made it to the blue-collar South back then.

Vicki Covington

Always smiling and never getting upset.
Keeping your composure to anyone. And
then when you get home, you cuss them
out.

> *Lady Chablis, of* Midnight in the Garden of Good
> and Evil *fame, on being asked what hospitality means to a*
> *Southern female impersonator*

**I'm not sitting here like some little woman
standing by my man like Tammy Wynette.**

> *Hillary Clinton, on* 60 Minutes *in the wake of her*
> *husband's sex scandal*

The naked body is one thing—but the
naked face, well, that is more than a
Southern woman can deal with.

> *Nanci Kincaid*

She didn't care what kind of mess you were, or what people were saying about you, or where your record was on the charts—she just saw another yearning soul standing there asking for love, whether you knew you were asking for it or not, and, by God, she was going to see that you got it.

Rosanne Cash, on Minnie Pearl

I'm as pure as the driven slush.

Tallulah Bankhead

In a good shoe, I wear a size six, but a seven feel so good, I buy a size eight.

Truvy Jones, in Robert Harling's Steel Magnolias

It is a special vanity of Southern women to believe that they are different from other American women.

Sharon McKern

Men on Women

Anyone who doesn't think there is a difference between Southern women and Yankee women has never dated a Southern woman *and* a Yankee woman.

Marc Smirnoff, Oxford American *editor*

While it is probably true that a Southern woman will take more bullcrap from her man than other women it's my impression (based on actual Southern women I know) that she will finally reach a breaking point, and when she does it will be more spectacular than the breaking point of other women.

John Berendt

The biggest myth about Southern women is that they wear too much makeup.

Peyton Manning

Yeah, I don't know, but I been around,
Tell me them Georgia women shake 'em on down.
Yes, I'm goin' Georgia line,
See if them women sweet like mine.

R. L. Burnside, "Georgia Women"

~~~~~

**Southern women hold you up to this thing,
which, you know, is your basic male standard.
Which is, you gotta be willing to die for things.**

Henry Allen

~~~~~

Southern women understand male pride.
Unlike Yankee women, they want you to
have some.

Henry Allen

He was sure any woman who would wordlessly volunteer to stretch bait so in the middle of a bream frenzy was the girl for him.

> *Padgett Powell, on a friend who married a Southern woman who, on their first date, had torn catalpa worms in half when they were running out of bait*

She was the South's Palladium, this Southern woman . . . the standard for its rallying, the mystic symbol of its nationality in face of the foe.

> *W. J. Cash*

J. E. B. Stuart in drag.

> *Fred Chappell, describing Scarlett O'Hara*

Southern women, on the whole, are a peculiar coy wine that does not travel well beyond its own indulgent clime. Northerners tend to find them faintly grotesque.

> *John Shelton Reed*

Anybody who wants to learn about the South should get to know her women.

James Dickey

I see them pass still, the little old tiny-headed women of Clinton, Mississippi, in the fifties, in their giant cars on the brick streets. Or on their porches or at their azalea beds scolding dogs, then me; nestled in the pews and bobbing heads in the aisles of the church. Bringing in their covered dishes to church suppers. They established the tone of my world.

Barry Hannah

The sweetness of Southern women often conceals the deadliness of snakes.

Pat Conroy, The Lords of Discipline

God made woman, made 'em mighty funny.
The lips 'round her mouth, just as sweet as any honey.

Mississippi John Hurt, "Salty Dog"

I said my honey my baby, don't put my love upon no shelf.
She said don't give me no lines and keep your hands to
yourself.

Georgia Satellites, "Keep Your Hands to Yourself"

**The women in the family represented good
sense and authority and our rebellion against the
situation formed us into a tight high-spirited
company.**

Fred Chappell, I Am One of You Forever

You know why I call [the Ole Miss coeds] goldfish? . . . If
you've ever watched a goldfish in a bowl, they love for you
to look at them, they dart around a lot, they don't think too
much, and they don't like to be still for very long, and then
when you put your hand down in the bowl to touch one of
them they swim away furiously.

Willie Morris

Men say they don't take women hunting because most women can't shoot worth a damn, but the real truth is men can't shoot worth a damn with women watching.

Vic Miller

We had the mill girls at Dream of Pines, too. . . . They'd look at you straightforwardly with either lust or disdain, and you could pick up on unknown swear words by just hanging back in a locker and listening to them crowd into the cafeteria line.

Barry Hannah, Geronimo Rex

The Southern Belle

The Belle is the ideal most frequently thrust upon young Southern women by hopeful mothers who persist, despite their own defeats, in believing that Eternal Youth is an attainable goal.

Donna Tartt

57
THE
SOUTHERN
WOMAN

Who has ever heard of "The Midwestern Lady," or "The Northern Belle?"

Gail Godwin

Driving a Honda Civic in a hoopskirt is no damn joke.

Diane Roberts, recalling the time she dressed as a Southern Belle for a costume party

I do like this job. I mean, it's a lot better than McDonald's. But it really gets hot sometimes. This bench I'm sitting on has, like, a fan underneath.

Melissa Todorovitch, on her job as a hoop-skirted "Southern Belle" at Florida's Cypress Gardens

It is the stupidest thing anybody ever had to do. And I sure as hell don't want to get into the position of romanticizing the Southern Belle. There's not a more imprisoning, ghastly stereotype.

Laura Freeman describing her career as a debutante

Lovely Ladies

Sheena Baby was LOVE, a sex-kitten goddess. I'd loved her for a long time . . . and I felt like I'd given part of myself away. Sheena Baby didn't hurt for me like I did for her. I knew it. I'd thought about shooting her first and me second, but that wouldn't have done either one of us any good.

Larry Brown, "Falling Out of Love"

I was dainty if I was anything, my mother saw to that. She wanted me to be pretty and did her damnedest to make me so.

Carson McCullers

Do not ever give a Queen a home appliance as a gift. Period. The end.

Jill Conner Browne, The Sweet Potato Queen's Book of Love

When I first met my SpottieOttieDopaliscious Angel,
I can remember that damn thang like yesterday.
The way she moved reminded me of a brown stallion horse
with skates on.

Outkast, "SpottieOttieDopaliscious"

**For women in the South, clothes, jewelry, the
way they wear their hair and do their makeup . . .
are part of a larger arsenal of feminine wiles.
They are the weapons of flirtation and glamour,
of power, class warfare, intimidation, and
seduction.**

Julia Reed

She's as sweet as Tupelo honey,
She's an angel in the first degree.

Van Morrison, "Tupelo Honey"

The Southern
Man

He should eat when he was hungry, drink when he was thirsty, dance when he was merry, vote for the candidate he liked best, and knock down any man who questioned his right to these privileges.

Reuben Davis, on the standard of conduct for men in antebellum Mississippi

Hair is the first thing. And teeth the second. Hair and teeth. A man got those two things he's got it all.

James Brown

Southern men didn't just scramble out of the primordial ooze in their four-by-four pickup trucks and start drinking beer and shooting squirrel right away. Oh, no, there's been a whole lot of evolution going on in Dixie in order for indigenous manhood to ascend to this current, sublime state of grace.

Gail Gilchriest, Bubbas and Beaus

Of all the properties which belong to honorable men, not one is so highly prized as that of character.

Henry Clay

The next time I feel the urge to get married, I think I'll just find a woman I hate and buy her a house.

Lewis Grizzard

When a woman has a flat tire on the expressway, all she has to do is step outside her car and stand. Within minutes, some male will stop and politely change the tire. Let a male try that. My hope is he has rations for a long stay.

Atlanta Journal-Constitution *columnist Ron Hudspeth*

It's a stingy man who pays the most in the end.

Robert E. Lee

Gentlemen

The gentlemanly idea, driven from England by Cromwell, had taken refuge in the South and fashioned for itself a world to its heart's desire: a world . . . wholly dominated by ideals of honor and chivalry and *noblesse*.

W. J. Cash, The Mind of the South

He grew extremely mellow in age, and liked to pass his time in company, arguing about predestination and infant damnation, proving conclusively that cotton was king and the damyankee didn't dare do anything about it, and developing a notable taste in the local liquors.

W. J. Cash, The Mind of the South

The Southern Gentleman speaks softly, slowly. He wears custom-tailored seersucker suits. He worships his ancestors, . . . he reads, he hunts, and he strictly adheres to the rituals of the civilized, daily cocktail hour.

Gail Gilchriest, Bubbas and Beaus

Maybe this is the romantic in me, but it seems that men were capable of passion in a way that we're afraid to be today. We're worried about being politically correct.

Georgia writer James Kilgo, comparing Southern men of the early 1900s to men of today

Rednecks and Good Ole Boys

You may be a redneck if . . . you have spent more on your pickup truck than on your education.

> *Jeff Foxworthy,* The Wit and Wisdom of Jeff Foxworthy

~~~~

God bless Merle Haggard. He actually did all the things Johnny Cash was supposed to have done.

> *Lewis Grizzard*

~~~~

The gentleman pulls trout from a babbling brook with fly tackle, while the Good Old Boy shocks catfish out of the bayou using dynamite or an old crank telephone.

> *Gail Gilchriest,* Bubbas and Beaus

Thanks to Louisiana's former governor Huey P. Long, all of us Southern boys have the right to believe that every man's a king.

Marty Stuart

A good ole boy is somebody that rides around in a pickup truck . . . and drinks beer and puts them in a litter bag. A redneck rides around in a pickup truck and drinks beer and throws them out the window.

Billy Carter

The redneck has an outlaw quality that the good old boy lacks, although the distinction is not hard and fast.

John Shelton Reed

Used as a disparaging term for a member of the white, rural laboring class, especially in the Southern United States.

American Heritage Dictionary's *definition of redneck*

Redneck Aristocrats, Good Old Boys, and Mean Sumbitches

Chapter title in B. C. Hall's and C. T. Wood's The South

〜〜〜

In Birmingham they love the governor,
Now we all did what we can do.
Watergate does not bother me,
Does your conscience bother you?

Lynard Skynard, "Sweet Home, Alabama"

〜〜〜

This can't be living. I drink too much Old Milwaukee and wake up in the morning and it tastes like old bread crusts in my mouth. All my underwear's dirty, I can't find my insurance policy.

Larry Brown, "The Apprentice"

A free and untrammeled white citizen of Alabama, who lives in the hills, has no means to speak of, dresses as he can, talks as he pleases, drinks whiskey when he gets it, and fires off his revolver as the fancy takes him.

Definition of "hillbilly," the first time this word appeared in print (1900)

Most of the . . . boys I knew at Ole Miss [were] passionless frat boys whose hearts had already narrowed and tightened (even at seventeen, eighteen, nineteen) into the hearts of the burghers and businessmen they would someday become.

Donna Tartt

Crackers are about as dumb as we treat 'em, and about two percent as inbred as the royal families over whom the civilized drool.

Dave Marsh

I know a real cowboy wouldn't think too much about manhandling a three-hundred-and-fifty-pound calf, but out here in Horn of Plenty, we're not real cowboys. We're just guys with cowshit on their boots.

Larry Brown

And I turned twenty-one in prison
doing life without parole.
No one could steer me right,
But Mama tried, Mama tried.

Johnny Cash, "Mama Tried"

Fightin'

Well I'd like to spit some Beech-Nut in that dude's eye
And shoot him in the head with my .45.

Hank Williams Jr., "Country Boy Can Survive"

Every once in a while, they had a fight, but it didn't hurt the attendance.

> *Luderin Darbone of the Hackberry Ramblers, on playing at the Silver Star in Louisiana in the 1930s and 1940s*

He had been a fearsome man, the kind of slim and lethal Southern man who would react with murderous fury when insulted, attacking with a knife or a pine knot or his bare hands.

> *Rick Bragg, on his father*

Each town had their little faction. They'd meet at each other's dances just to fight. . . . That was just the thing to do.

> *Guitarist Harold Cavallero, on playing honky-tonks in rural Louisiana*

In the younger days of the Republic, there lived in the county of ———, two men, who were admitted on all hands to be the very best men in the county—which, in the Georgia vocabulary, means they could flog any other two men in the county.

Augustus Baldwin Longstreet, Georgia Scenes

We spoke boastfully in bass voices; we used the word "nigger" to prove tough fiber of our feelings; we spouted excessive profanity as a sign of our coming manhood.

Richard Wright, Black Boy

It was common, acceptable, not to be able to read, but a man who wouldn't fight, couldn't fight, was a pathetic thing. To be afraid was shameful. I'm not saying I agree with it. It's just the way it was.

Rick Bragg

"The Race Question"

You can be up to your boobies in white satin, with gardenias in your hair and no sugar cane for miles, but you can still be working on a plantation.

Billie Holiday

Being Black in the South

The South is, in a sense, the myth in the landscape of Black America.

Eugenia Collier

People in Stamps used to say that the whites in our town were so prejudiced that a Negro couldn't buy vanilla ice cream.

Maya Angelou

If you go in a store, you didn't say, "Gimme a can of Prince Albert." Not with that white man on the can. You said, "Gimme a can of Mister Prince Albert."

Memphis Slim

I am not ashamed of my grandparents for having been slaves. I am only ashamed of myself for having at one time been ashamed.

Ralph Ellison, Invisible Man

Go to work in the morning, you know, 'bout 4 o'clock.
Uh, if the mule don't holler, yeah, I don't know when to
   stop.
Down in Mississippi, baby, uh whoa yeah, where the cotton
   grow tall.

Jimmy Reed, "Down in Mississippi"

A Negro who migrates South is as rare as a Jew seeking transportation to Berlin.

George S. Schuyler

The Southern white man has always been more honest about segregation than the Northern white man. The Northern white man claimed the barriers were down, but they were very much up. But the Southern white man let you know in no uncertain terms, "Nigger, I don't want you eatin' in my business."

Martin Luther King Jr.

In order to find Africa, you don't have to go back to Africa. All you have to do is go back to the South.

August Wilson

Racism exists everywhere, but in the North, they're just nastier about it.

Tamara Jeffries

God bless you all. I am a innocent man.

The epitaph on the tombstone of Ed Johnson,
who was lynched in Chatanooga in 1906

In our culture we're just ate up with what I call skin hang-ups. I'm glad I'm in the Hall of Fame. I'm glad I'm right next to the people that I love—Ernest Tubb, Marty Robbins, the whole bit. I don't care if they're pink.

Charley Pride, on being inducted into the Country Music
Hall of Fame

My great-grandfather . . . was the first black political candidate in the state of Mississippi. He ran for the border and made it. And the reason he ran for the border, he said, was that the people were very clannish. He didn't mind them having hang-ups, he just didn't want to be one of their hang-ups.

Redd Foxx

One day, while at work in the coal-mine, I happened to overhear two miners talking about a great school for coloured people somewhere in Virginia. . . . As they went on describing the school, it seemed to me that it must be the greatest place on earth, and not even Heaven presented more attractions for me at that time than did the Hampton Normal and Agricultural Institute in Virginia.

Booker T. Washington

Booker T. Washington will suit us.
Send him at once.

*Telegram from the founders of the Tuskegee Institute, indicating
they could accept a black man to head their new school*

In the South . . . churchgoing men went home to their wives every night, paid their tax on time. . . . They didn't have anything wrong with them, other than they hung black people on the weekends and ran Jews out of town.

Al Sharpton

Some of those stories he wrote weren't about white folks, they were about black folks, and everybody knew that in Oxford.

Lloyd Johnson, William Faulkner's paperboy

"Social responsibility, sir," I said.

"You weren't being smart, were you, boy?" he said, not unkindly.

"No, sir!"

"You sure that about equality was a mistake?"

"Oh, yes, sir," I said. "I was swallowing blood."

Ralph Ellison, Invisible Man

White Americans might understand and show more compassion toward the problems of blacks in New York, Chicago, Miami, and Los Angeles were they to admit that many of those situations are best understood as continuations of the tragedy of the South.

Anthony Walton

All I was doing was trying to get home from work.

Rosa Parks

I think his starting premise was from a sociological perspective and mine tends to be from a psychological perspective. Nowadays we're dealing with people who are so crushed by life that we've got to help mend their spirits so they have the strength to rise up and change the economic and the social conditions.

> *Rev. Bernice King, daughter of Martin Luther King Jr., on how her work differs from her father's*

Black Americans are no more angry today than they have ever been. The difference is, they can now talk back, or yell back if they want to, where fifty years ago it would have led to a lynch mob.

Will Campbell

A lot of what's going on in our society today that's seen as real or on the cutting edge . . . has a high level of Uncle Tom in it, too. All the gold teeth and the over-ghettoing, you can't get much more Tomin' than that.

Wynton Marsalis, on the opinion that Louis Armstrong was an Uncle Tom

We hold that freedom is the natural right of all men, which they themselves have no more right to give or barter away than they have to sell their honor, their wives, or their children.

From a letter from fifty-nine black citizens of Tennessee to the Union Convention of Tennessee, 1865

How big does a person have to grow in this part of the country before he's going to stand up and say, "Let us stop treating other men and women and children with such cruelty just because they are born colored?"

Mahalia Jackson

I have a dream that my four little children will one day live in a nation where they will not be judged by the color of their skin, but by the content of their character.

Martin Luther King Jr.

White Views on Race

Race is like a big crazy cousin locked in the basement, a red-eyed giant who strangled a dog and crippled a policeman the last time he got loose. We never forget that he's down there. But it's amazing how long we can ignore him, no matter how much noise he makes moaning and banging on the pipes.

Hal Crowther

Crackers never did admit that they were oppressors. They could always put that off on Washington.

Roy Blount Jr.

I had joined the Klan because of those robes. They made good copy, you know. Good pictures.

David Duke

Nigger, your breed ain't metaphysical.

Robert Penn Warren, in a 1945 poem

Cracker, your breed ain't exegetical.

Sterling A. Brown's response to the above

The colored girls danced with the white boys, and the colored boys danced with the white girls. We hugged each other's neck. If you had been at the beach during that period of time, you'd have thought segregation didn't exist.

Leon Williams (aka "Rubber Legs"), on R&B—and the dancing it inspired—in the 1940s and 1950s

Southerners are more lonely and estranged, I think because we have lived so long in an artificial social system that we insisted was natural and right and just—when all along we knew it wasn't.

Carson McCullers

When a black man and a white man meet, neither man knows where the other is located in the journey against prejudice. But when the two men realize that each has made that journey, then there's a real bond. And that bond is stronger in the South than you'll find anywhere else in the country.

Al Gore

As a dispenser of facts and biases to university students, I keep running into undergraduates who can't quite believe that things were really as bad, racially, in the South thirty or forty years ago as they are said to have been.

Fred Hobson

My aunt leaned down and put her arm around my shoulders. Her great soft breast pressed warmly against my ear. She said: "No, son. Robert Jones is a nigger. You don't say 'mister' when you speak of a nigger. You don't say 'Mr. Jones,' you say 'nigger Jones.'"

Harry Crews

We share the South now publicly, eat together, even marry, but there is still a distance, a final separation that will never end.

Tim McLaurin

A Southerner looks at a Negro twice: once when he is a child and sees his nurse for the first time; second, when he is dying and there is a Negro with him to change his bedclothes. But he does not look at him in the sixty years in between. And so he knows as little about Negroes as he does about Martians, less, because he knows that he does not know about Martians.

Walker Percy, The Last Gentleman

The Civil Rights Movement and Beyond

Two, four, six, eight.
We ain't gonna integrate.
Eight, six, four, two.
Bet you sons-of-bitches do.

Jump-rope rhyme recorded among black children in east Texas

In the local courthouses and on the TV news,
where it counted, [the Civil Rights movement]
was a struggle to prove who were the truest
fundamentalists, black ones or white ones.

Roy Blount Jr.

I have ceased to think in terms of race: I
think only in terms of the individuals.

Zora Neale Hurston

Weary feet and weary souls were lightened. It was such a night. We didn't have to walk no more. Even before Martin Luther King got up and told us it was over, we knew it was over, and we knew we had won.

> *Georgia Gilmore, on the meeting celebrating the success of the Montgomery bus boycott*

We don't need the U.S. Army at Ole Miss or fire hoses in Birmingham to fight out our beliefs on racial equality; now we squabble endlessly over affirmative action, welfare, and the criminal justice system.

> *Anthony Walton*

No one here today would pretend the Old South is dead, that the events of the past twenty-five years, even my presence here today, has transformed our peculiar world beyond recognition. The Confederate flag still flies in place on this campus.

> *Charlayne Hunter-Gault*

Well a nigga uneducated, integrated,
Thinkin' "We shall overcome."
But a nigga tryin' to be white is what it seem
like a nigga has become.

Cee-Lo, of Atlanta rap group Goodie Mob

The problems we are facing in the American society are not problems that were created yesterday . . . and they're not going to be solved in the matter of a few days or a few weeks or a few months or maybe a few years. But you have to take the long hard look and do what you can do, but do something. Be involved.

Georgia Congressman and Civil Rights veteran John Lewis

I had felt for a long time that if I was ever told
to get up so a white person could sit, that I
would refuse to do so.

Rosa Parks

What really happened in the Meredith case when the state decided to resist was that they were playing out the last chapter of the Civil War.

> *Constance Baker Motley, James Meridith's attorney, on the integration of Ole Miss*

"Mississippi" is perhaps the most loaded proper noun in American English.

> *Anthony Walton*

The more visible signs of protest are gone, but I think there is a realization that the tactics of the late-sixties are not sufficient to meet the challenges of the seventies.

> *Coretta Scott King*

I had crossed the line. I was free; but there was no one to welcome me to the land of freedom. I was a stranger in a strange land.

> *Harriet Tubman*

Many whites, even white Southerners, told me that even though it may have seemed like the blacks were being freed, they felt more free and at ease themselves.

Rosa Parks

Now question—Is every nigga wit dreads for the cause? Is every nigga with golds for the fall? Naw.

Outkast, "Aquemini"

Martin Luther King Jr.

I have a dream that one day this nation will rise up, live out the true meaning of its creed: we hold these truths to be self evident, that all men are created equal.

Martin Luther King Jr.

I want to be the white man's brother, not his brother-in-law.

Martin Luther King Jr.

When I marched with Martin Luther King in Selma, I felt my legs were praying.

Rabbi Abraham Heschel

Injustice anywhere is a threat to justice everywhere.

Martin Luther King Jr.

We know through painful experience that freedom is never voluntarily given by the oppressor; it must be demanded by the oppressed.

Martin Luther King Jr.

I was working in a steel mill in Chicago when I heard this minister on the radio. His name was Martin Luther King Jr., and he was saying what I wanted to say and was saying it like I wanted to say it.

"Pops" Staples, of the Staple Singers

89
"THE
RACE
QUESTION"

The nations of Asia and Africa are moving with jetlike
speed toward gaining political independence, but we still
creep at horse-and-buggy pace toward gaining a cup of
coffee at a lunch counter.

Martin Luther King Jr.

**I have almost reached the regrettable conclusion
that the Negro's great stumbling block in his
stride toward freedom is not the White Citizen's
Counciler or the Ku Klux Klanner, but the white
moderate, who is more devoted to "order"
than to justice.**

Martin Luther King Jr.

Returning violence for violence multiplies
violence, adding deeper darkness to a
night already devoid of stars.

Martin Luther King Jr.

Southern Culture

You think I don't have culture just because I'm from down in Georgia. Believe me, we got culture there. We've always had sushi. We just used to call it *bait.*

Ben Jones

Society, Customs, and Traditions

You eat a possum, you bare [bury] its eyes. . . . Possums eat whatall's dead. You gone die too, boy. . . . You be dead an in the ground, but you eat this possum an he gone come looking for you.

Auntie, in Harry Crews's A Childhood

Every Southerner alive, at many, many points in his or her childhood, heard the words, "But what will people think?"

Julia Reed

Among the great democracies of the world, the Southern
states remain the chief considerable area in which an
extremely small proportion of the citizens vote.

V. O. Key

**In the South of my youth, there were only two
kinds of men: those who drove Fords and those
who drove Chevrolets.**

Ludlow Porch

An unscientific statistic: Somewhere between one-third and
one-half of the men who choose to have their weddings
performed by a public servant in Brevard County, Florida,
also wear baseball caps during the ceremony.

*Gary White, former clerk at the Brevard County court
records department, whose job description included performing
marriages*

My greatest instinct is to be free. I found that in New Orleans.

Tennessee Williams

When people from the South ask that question they don't necessarily mean geography. They may mean family, neighborhood, time.

Beverly Lowry, on the question "Where are you from?"

Nearly everybody I knew had something missing, a finger cut off, a toe split, an ear half-chewed away, an eye clouded with blindness from a glancing fence staple. And if they didn't have something missing, they were carrying scars from barbed wire, or knives, or fishhooks.

Harry Crews

Where, outside the South, is there a society that believes even covertly in the Code of Honor?

Allen Tate

In Monroeville, they're Southern people, and if they know
you are working at home they think nothing of walking
right in for coffee. But they wouldn't dream of interrupting
you on the golf course.

Harper Lee

**The South is unique on this continent for
having founded and defended a culture which
was according to the European principles of
culture.**

John Crowe Ransom

The greatest of all privileges is the
privilege of being let alone.

Donald Davidson

I'm out there in the fields, you know, pickin' beans and all. You have to do that when you go down there. That's the punishment, you know.

David Kimbrough, on his time in Mississippi's Parchman Penitentiary

My husband, Dennis, liked these hill people and the raw sensuality he saw in them. I think he wanted to be like them. He wanted weeds in his yard, a walleyed child with a bouquet of dandelions, a rust-eaten car that would take him nowhere.

Vicki Covington

Washington, D.C., perfectly combines Southern efficiency with Northern charm.

John F. Kennedy

It is said that the first thing one is asked in Atlanta is "What do you do?"; in Charleston, "Who were your ancestors?"; and in Savannah, "What would you like to drink?"

> *Rosemary Daniell,* Sleeping with Soldiers: In Search of the Macho Man

I have always been struck by the way people love New Orleans. They love it the way people love Paris.

Tom Piazza

Louisiana was alarming and peculiar anyway. There were plenty of Catholics, many seemed touched by at least mild cases of voodoo, and adults went public with their gaudiest dreams.

Barry Hannah

The federal government ought to strike a medal for the Sears, Roebuck company for sending all those catalogues to farming families, for bringing all that color and all that mystery and all that beauty into the lives of country people.

Harry Crews

I don't want realism. I want magic!

Blanche DuBois, in Tennessee Williams's A Streetcar Named Desire

A real trader don't never find nothing that he can't use. If he is a trader—and you're looking at one now—he will trade you for anything you've got. If he can't use it, he'll find someone else that can.

Businessman, auctioneer, and Southern character Ray Lum

EVOLUTIONISTS COME FROM MONKEYS

Sign on the road outside of Dayton, Tennessee, home of the Scopes Trial Festival

New Orleans is both intimately related to the South and yet in a real sense cut adrift not only from the South but the rest of Louisiana. . . . A proper enough American city and yet within the next few hours the tourist is apt to see more nuns and naked women than he ever saw before.

Walker Percy

It vexed my grandmother's conscience to see someone sit down and take an easy smoke. The sight of someone not working for a moment or two caused great catalogs of useless tasks to fret her mind.

Fred Chappell, I Am One of You Forever

Auntie had tanned the hides by rubbing the animals' hides on the flesh side with their brains. It caused the hair to fall out of the hide and left it soft and pliable.

Harry Crews

Guilt was and is today the biggest crop raised in Dixie, harvested each summer just before cotton is picked.

Lillian Smith

He passed more and more cars which had Confederate plates on the front bumper and plastic Christs on the dashboard.

Walker Percy, The Last Gentleman

I had some beer iced down in the trunk. They got a crazy law in this county. You can't go into a store and buy cold beer; you can only buy it hot. So you have to get a cooler and keep it in the car. You have to always be thinking ahead.

Larry Brown, "Wild Thing"

repeated

Manners

Manners are the mask of decency that we employ at need, the currency of fair communication.

Stark Young, I'll Take My Stand

Manners are essential and are essentially moral.

William Alexander Percy

The Southern Negro has the most beautiful manners in the world, and the Southern white, learning from him, I suspect, is a close second.

William Alexander Percy

We say grace, and we say ma'am.
If you ain't into that we don't give a damn.

Hank Williams Jr., "Country Boy Can Survive"

Think Martha Stewart meets the
Southern Belle Primer

> *Laura Winner, in* The Oxford American, *describing*
> Southern Lady *magazine*

~~~~

**Any man should know enough to get up and
walk around while he waited.**

> *Eudora Welty, "Death of a Traveling Salesman"*

~~~~

"Start back," he said, almost formally. "Ain't no need for us
to drink outdoors, like hogs."

> *Eudora Welty, "Death of a Travelling Salesman"*

~~~~

Southerners will be polite until they are
angry enough to kill you.

> *John Shelton Reed*

Our idea was to invite representatives of all the groups to a covered dish dinner, thinking that regardless of race or politics or whatever, Southerners have always been brought up to be nice at the table.

Maggie Ray

I don't know what class is, but I can tell when one has it. You can tell it from a mile away.

Bear Bryant

In Charleston, even traffic jams are characterized by an "oh, no, you go first" quality.

Blanche McCrary Boyd

Fashion

No self-respecting Memphis girl would be caught dead in an airport, about the most public of places after all, in wrinkled clothes and messy hair, without makeup or jewelry, no matter how good-looking she might be.

Julia Reed

~~~~

When people looked at us Southern wives coming to those football games in six-degree weather with our well-accessorized, color-coordinated outfits, helmet hair, and painted fingernails, they stared like we were in a freak show.

Nanci Kincaid, on college football games in Wyoming

~~~~

My beloved red shoes were cut so low you could see the cracks of my toes, and had a blocky Spanish dancing heel, thin ankle straps and little floweredy cutouts in the leather. Whore shoes, my father would have said.

Beverly Lowry

We sleep in earrings in the South.

A woman from Atlanta speaking to Vogue *about the Southern sense of fashion*

I must have been five or six. There were the cows and livestock and the scuppernong vines trailing over the arbor. It was immaculately clean and everything was in its proper place. Most thoughtfully, all the hens were in their little nests in the shade of a chinaberry tree. [The family servant] wanted me to touch one, to feel the egg and the hen's down. And I realized this was my first reach into sensuality. Because the eggs were warm. It was the shape and hardness—the softness—of the feathers, all at the same time. I was frozen with the sensation.

Fashion designer Geoffrey Beene, describing his family's Louisiana farm

Like an elegant Southern garden warmed by the sun.

What "Southernness" smells like, according to Benn Johnson, creator of Southernness perfume

Dogs

Sam and I talked a lot together, had long and involved conversations, mostly about which one of us had done the other one wrong and, if not about that, about which one of us was the better man. It would be a good long time before I started thinking of Sam as a dog instead of a person.

Harry Crews

Dogs never make nasty comments the way some people do and they don't have to be excused from the room if they need to fart.

Larry Brown

My *dog* died. I went out there in the yard and looked at him and there he was, dead as a hammer. Boy, I hated it. I knew I'd have to look around and see about a shovel.

Larry Brown, "Big Bad Love"

The dog of your boyhood teaches you a great deal about friendship, and love, and death: Old Skip was my brother.

Willie Morris, My Dog Skip

You could talk to him as well as you could to many human beings, and *much* better than you could to some.

Willie Morris, My Dog Skip

A yard dog is the best dog to have. Yard dogs spend their days under trucks to stay out of the hot sun, and they are recognizable by the oil and grease on their backs and by the humble way they walk sideways toward the individual calling them.

Lewis Grizzard

He's a springer spaniel with brain damage. He got shut up too many times in a hot car. I'm training him to get my Copenhagen, though.

Former Atlanta Falcon Billy Ryckman

Southern Religion

The Bible Belt likes its religion the same as its whiskey—strong, homemade, and none too subtle.

Anonymous

Religion in Society

My fundamental principle would be . . . that we are saved by our good works, which are within our power, and not by our faith, which is not in our power.

Thomas Jefferson

People who haven't grown up in the South, in the Bible Belt particularly, have little understanding of how much a part of the fabric of Southern life religion is.

Barry Moser

I've never detected any conflict between God's will and my political duty. If you violate one, you violate the other.

Jimmy Carter

It seemed unreasonable that the one time government acknowledged God's existence would be in response to something that killed twenty-five people.

> *Arkansas Governor and Baptist minister Mike Huckabee, on why he refused to sign legislation that referred to a tornado that had blown through his state as an "act of God"*

I'm just as much of a Baptist as he is.

> *Arkansas State Representative Shane Broadway, whose district was hit by the aforementioned tornado*

I think it is safe to say that while the South is hardly Christ-centered, it is most certainly Christ-haunted.

Flannery O'Connor

In a small town like Banner, if the Baptists couldn't be against the Methodists, they'd have nothing to talk about.

Eudora Welty

~~~~

Religion is a very important part of my life. I think I feel somewhat more comfortable speaking in the rhymes of my faith in my speeches when I'm home in the South than I do in other places.

Bill Clinton

~~~~

I'm sure the ACLU leadership here in New York view themselves as cutting edge and the little school in Mississippi as a last ditch resistance to the notion of a secular society. This is a grave misreading. Rather, the little school in Mississippi is the cutting edge, and the ACLU is the last ditch resistance in defending the notion of a secular America.

Father Richard John Neuhaus, on the intercom prayer lawsuit in Pontotoc, Mississippi

Kids in Ecru, Mississippi, go to Bible drills and missionary clubs and summer camps like kids in the suburbs of Atlanta go to soccer practice or piano lessons.

Stacy Mattingly, on the intercom prayer lawsuit in Mississippi

Nowhere else, perhaps, have the rich seedbeds of Western homes found such a growing climate for guilt as is produced in the South by the combination of a warm moist evangelism and racial segregation.

Lillian Smith

When I was suddenly catapulted into the leadership of the bus protest in Montgomery, Alabama, I felt we would be supported by the white church. I felt that the white ministers, priests and rabbis of the South would be among our strongest allies. Instead, some have been outright opponents.

Martin Luther King Jr.

He had got used to good steady wistful post-Protestant Yankees . . . and here all at once he found himself among as light-footed and as hawk-eyed and God-fearing a crew as one could imagine. Everyone went to church and was funny and clever and sensitive in the bargain.

> *Walker Percy,* The Last Gentleman

Mama wanted me to be a preacher. I told her coachin' and preachin' were a lot alike.

> *Bear Bryant*

If, sadly, institutions like the Methodist Church cannot see through their ideological fog and make this affirmation, I say be done with them. They need Emory more than Emory needs them.

III
SOUTHERN
RELIGION

> *Alex DeGood, in a student newspaper editorial, on Emory University's refusal to allow a gay marriage in its chapel*

Conscious of the far mission fields but not the world.

Barry Hannah, describing the Baptist college he attended in Mississippi

Race—I think it's more deeply embedded in people in the South and so, in that vein, we've not done the job of being God's representatives of the Church. We are seriously divided.

Rev. Bernice King, on being asked what is the most pressing religious issue facing the South

We knew we had been dealt an injustice, so we thought that truth was relative to us. We had been done wrong, so let's thump. Since Islam, I understand that truth is not relative. Truth is universal.

Jamil Abdullah Al-Amin (formerly H. Rap Brown)

Faith and Spirituality

Some people say, "Well, I don't know what's going to be at the end." I don't either, but I'll tell you what, I don't want to take no chances.

Rev. Willie Morganfield

I have great faith in God. And I've always felt like I've been on a little higher spiritual plane because I pray all the time. And I just reach up, crawl under the wings of angels, and press on.

June Carter Cash

Christian teachings, Christian mysteries, not the church, have stayed important to me. My thinking was totally shaped by the notion of a Jesus who lived a legendary life and died for people's sins. I don't think I'll ever shake those very powerful Bible stories that I got so often and so young that they've become part of how I write.

Jim Grimsley

Search for faith doesn't exactly say what I am trying to say, it's a search for the nature of belief.

Harry Crews

I cannot tell you why, born in France, my journey ended here. I have tried to go further but I cannot. It makes no difference.

Thomas Merton, on setting up his monastery in rural Kentucky

Every night I watched Granny turn out the light and get down on her knees beside the bed. She crosses her hands on the mattress and laid her head on her hands. She prayed silently, without moving. . . . I tried to stay awake to see how long she prayed . . . but I always fell asleep before she said Amen.

Tony Earley

Allah divides mankind only on the basis of belief, not on the basis of race, or any other physiological characteristics. There are only believers and nonbelievers.

Jamil Abdullah Al-Amin (formerly H. Rap Brown)

Auntie made me believe we live in a discoverable world, but that most of what we discover is an unfathomable mystery that we can name—even defend against—but never understand.

Harry Crews

Never be too proud to get down on your knees and pray.

Bear Bryant

116

THE
QUOTABLE
SOUTH

I've looked on a lot of women with lust. I've committed adultery in my heart many times. This is something God recognizes I will do—and I have done it—and God forgives me for it.

Jimmy Carter

I think it pisses God off if you walk by the color purple in a field somewhere and don't notice it.

Alice Walker, The Color Purple

Church

What is so influential in the South is not Jesus Christ, but rather the social anchor represented by the church.

Alan Jacobs

In South Georgia people act like the First Commandment is, "Thou shalt go to church," and the Second Commandment is, "Thou shalt get others to go to church."

Millard Fuller

Church was our town—come together not to kneel and worship but to see each other.

Lillian Smith

If you ask a Southerner why he or she goes to church . . . you're liable to receive a blank look implying, "What else would I do?"

Alan Jacobs

I would be hard pressed to recall even a single sentence from the hundreds of sermons I heard growing up, but I can sing from memory at least one verse from each of the hymns we sang from the *Broadman Hymnal*.

Tony Earley

Singing is to preaching what gravy is to steak. Gravy is not steak, but it makes the steak taste better.

Rev. Willie Morganfield

My life's been hard since I finished grad school, and the church has been there for me. But it compartmentalized me away from all the things that used to bring me joy—weirdos, dreaming, fun. It made me kind of righteous and judgmental.

Georgia artist Terry Rowlett

It was Sunday, bright and hot, and we were on the way to church. Everybody except daddy, who was sick from whiskey. But he would not have gone even if he were well. The few times he ever did go he could never stand more than five or ten minutes of the sermon before he quietly went out a side door to stand beside the pickup truck smoking hand-rolled Prince Albert cigarettes until it was all over.

Harry Crews

The Bible Belt

There are few artists today who would dare probe so ruthlessly the raw sores of our life as did these evangelists.

Lillian Smith, on the preachers at camp meetings

I consider myself 40 percent Catholic and 60 percent Baptist . . . but I'm in favor of *every* religion, with the possible exception of snake-chunking.

Earl Long

What a different breed [the Episcopalians] had been from their Methodist and Presbyterian contemporaries. They danced and they played cards, of course, and they drank whiskey, and they did just about whatever they wanted on Sunday. They indulged in what their Baptist neighbors called "that barbarous ritual, infant baptism."

Peter Taylor, "The Decline and Fall of the Episcopal Church"

The spirit within the churches was not so different. We Methodists just didn't speak in tongues, and prior to Communion we didn't handle rattlesnakes.

Dennis Covington

You can't curb a Baptist. Let them in and you can't keep 'em down, when somebody dies.

Mrs. Pease, in Eudora Welty's The Optimist's Daughter

A cesspool of Baptists, a miasma of Methodism, snake charmers, . . . and syphilitic evangelists.

H. L. Mencken, describing the South

The Baptists and Methodists emerged in the decades after the Revolution as the South's strongest evangelical churches, in part because both groups dispensed with a formally educated clergy. They regarded inner claims to divine appointment as sufficient authorization.

> *Christine Leigh Heyrman,* Southern Cross: The Beginnings of the Bible Belt

Baptists never make love standing up. They're afraid someone might see them and think they're dancing.

> *Lewis Grizzard*

When I get up to preach, all I do is to knock out the bung and let nature cut her caper.

> *Rev. Sam Jones, well-known preacher in the South after the Civil War*

SOUTHERN
RELIGION

The fancied home of the cavalier is the home of the nearest approach to Puritanism and to the most vital protestant evangelicalism in the world to-day.

Edwin A. Alderman

Gettin' Saved

It's such a con job. I knew men and women who were geniunely evil, who had this little secret— on their deathbed they would embrace Jesus and it would all be okay. It ain't okay.

Dorothy Allison

What I remember most from that night is the sight of both my grandmothers on their knees, crying and begging me to join them at the altar. They were afraid that I would die without being saved, that I would spend eternity crying out in hell for God to save me.

Tony Earley, describing a revival from his childhood

I come up out of that altar, praisin' God, tears rollin' from my eyes . . . hollerin' and praisin' God.

Rev. Howard Finster, on the night he was saved

I felt that same power, Lord.
My soul caught on fire.
I'm just glad he stopped by in Alabama.
The Lord stopped by, one Tuesday evening,
Blessed my soul and gone.

Dorothy Love Coates, "Strange Man"

Televangelism

I just want to lobby for God.

Billy Graham, on establishing national headquarters in Washington

The South's most influential clergyman, by virtue of pulpit power and personal integrity, Billy Graham is a former Fuller Brush salesman who baits his hook with as little theology as any of God's fisherman.

Hal Crowther

The first time I saw Jim and Tammy Faye Bakker, I swear I thought they were two male comics from Long Island doing a brilliant send-up of televangelism.

Hal Crowther

Preachers are not called to be politicians, but to be soul winners.

Jerry Falwell

If we had more hell in the pulpit, we would have less hell in the pew.

Billy Graham

> The idea that religion and politics don't mix was invented by the devil.
>
> *Jerry Falwell*

Non-Believers, Sinners, and Other Blasphemers

My daddy, Henry Oochee May, had a penchant for that trinity of Southern sin: whiskey, women, and music.

Connie May Fowler

Early this mornin', ooh, when you knocked upon my door
And I said, "Hello, Satan, I believe it's time to go."

Robert Johnson, "Me and the Devil Blues"

I picked up the rhythms of Scripture for my tales, I'm certain, but it was mystery and sin that had me. . . . In Baptist songs I always liked where you were a wretch or a worm or, just as I am, hopeless.

Barry Hannah

[Southerners] believe more in the reality of Satan than in the reality of God.

Episcopal bishop Robert R. Brown

When I was a kid Uncle Remus put me to bed,
With a picture of Stonewall Jackson above my head.
Then Daddy came in to kiss his little man
With gin on his breath and a Bible in his hand.

Bob McDill

He was dead a long time before Nietzsche said God is dead. God is dead because this is a secular world we live in. . . . That somehow offends me, really deeply offends me that it's a secular world.

Harry Crews

It's Sunday school. Some teacher from a local church is coming in and teaching his or her religious point of view.

Lisa Herdahl, who filed a federal lawsuit against the Pontotoc County, Florida, school district to stop students from praying and reading scripture over the intercom

I think that whenever two or three people gather in God's name, it's only a matter of time before they start trouble.

Tony Earley

Visions, Awakenin', and Moanin'

Sometimes I feel like moanin', and I feel like moanin' tonight. Because when I'm moanin' the devil don't know what I'm talking about.

Rev. Al Green, during a gospel concert in New York City

It has always seemed to me that I was not so much born into this life as I awakened to it.

Harry Crews

The first time, I saw the sun spin. The second time, we saw gold flakes fall from the sky. The third time, my son took a photograph of the sky—it's a clear picture of the Blessed Mother.

Jan Martinez, on visiting the Conyers, Georgia, home of Nancy Fowler, to whom some claim the Virgin Mary appears once a year

Southern Politics

When you have the facts on your side, argue the facts. When you have the law on your side, argue the law. When you have neither, holler.

Al Gore

The Parties

[The Democratic Party] was the party of the South. . . . To question it in any detail, was *ipso facto* to stand branded as a renegade to race, to country, to God, and to Southern Womanhood.

W. J. Cash

The difference between a national Democrat and an Alabama Democrat is like the difference between a Communist and a non-Communist.

George Wallace

I know I get shoes, I get clothes, when the Democrats get
back in again.
Vote them, they vote them in, I'm a Democrat man, I'm a
Democrat man.

John Lee Hooker, "Democrat Man"

**I suspect some of the reason we stayed
Democrats is because we have *always* been
Democrats. It's part of our core identity, like
being protestants, and part of our culture, like
eating fried catfish and watching college football.**

*Diane Roberts, on the persistence of the Democratic Party in
her Southern family*

My old daddy was a Republican, like his own daddy before
him. I don't know how they ever come to be so. But I know,
sure God, it never done them no good hereabouts.

*Sam Flemming, in Peter Taylor's "The Decline and Fall of
the Episcopal Church"*

Most of the South now belongs to the party of Lincoln, which takes its marching orders directly from Wall Street.

Hal Crowther

The Issues

The basic ingredients of Southern politics have always been emotions and attitudes about race.

Albert Gore Sr., Let the Glory Out:
My South and Its Politics

When the scales are weighted in favor of one gender or one race or one privileged background, no one in a democracy is well-served.

Ann Richards, former governor of Texas

I don't think you can get a vote like this on a horse trade. You get this one on conscience.

Georgia Senate Majority Leader Charles Walker, arguing that lobbying efforts would not decide the upcoming vote to change Georgia's state flag

We are concerned not only about the Negro poor, but the poor all over America and all over the world. Every man deserves a right to a job or an income so that he can pursue liberty, life, and happiness.

Coretta Scott King

I draw the line in the dust and toss the gauntlet before the feet of tyranny, and I say segregation now, segregation tomorrow, segregation forever.

George Wallace

I'm not saying that Patrick Sonnier or any of the condemned killers I've accompanied were heroes. I do not glorify them. I do not condone their terrible crimes. But each of these men was a human being and each had a transcendence, a dignity, which should assure them of two very basic human rights that the United Nations Universal Declaration of Human Rights calls for: the right not to be tortured, the right not to be killed.

Sister Helen Prejean, Dead Man Walking

Whenever the Constitution comes between me and the virtues of the women of the South, I say to hell with the Constitution.

Former Mississippi governor and U.S. senator Theodore Bilbo

Anyone can see that the tops of our mountains are missing, and everyone knows who let it happen.

Denise Giardina, West Virginia novelist and opponent of mountaintop-removal mining

In modern Southern politics, race has virtually disappeared as an issue. It is being replaced by an equally traditional Southern issue of economic class against economic class, the politics dramatized by Huey Long.

David Leon Chandler, The Natural Superiority of Southern Politicians

Presidents

He's smart, funny, a good guy. He's bad to stay out late and chase women.

> *A description of Bill Clinton by a reporter who'd been covering him since his first term as governor of Arkansas, as told to Roy Blount Jr.*

The metaphor of Clinton as Elvis is powerful because of a sense that we may be able to catch what we want from this man, what we hope for and what we most fear, if we think of him as a version of Elvis Presley rather than merely as himself.

> *Greil Marcus,* Double Trouble: Bill Clinton and Elvis Presley in a Land of No Alternatives

Yes, I tried marijuana in England, but I didn't like it. And I didn't inhale.

Bill Clinton

The first symbolic event in the mythology of the contemporary South was the election of Jimmy Carter in 1976.

Stephen A. Smith

I am determined that at the end of this administration we shall be able to stand up anywhere in the world—in New York, California, or Florida—and say "I'm a Georgian," and be proud of it.

Jimmy Carter

Human rights is the soul of our foreign policy, because human rights is the very soul of our sense of nationhood.

Jimmy Carter

The experience of democracy is like the experience of life itself—always changing, infinite in its variety, sometimes turbulent and all the more valuable for having been tested by adversity.

Jimmy Carter

Politicians

We raised him for it. I taught him to work hard and do his duty, and his mother made sure he studied his lessons.

Albert Gore Sr., on hearing Bill Clinton picked his son as his running mate

I looked that up: It means *redneck*.

Florida politician Donald Tucker, on being called a "provincial agrarian" by the Miami Herald

It is good to be home in the state of great people, warm hospitality, and conservative voters—if only the rest of America was as perfect as South Carolina.

> *Strom Thurmond, at the 1996 South Carolina Republican Convention*

He's a monstrous mascot, a gross pet we keep in the spirit people keep pythons and ferrets. Tarheels will re-elect him as long as he can throw the Eastern media into apoplexy.

> *Hal Crowther, describing North Carolina senator Jesse Helms*

George Wallace is dishing out his politics the way many of his fellow Alabamians like their whiskey and religion—as hot and raw as white lightnin' and as primitive as Baptist fundamentalism.

> *James R. Dickinson*

THE
QUOTABLE
SOUTH

You don't have to get snippy.

Al Gore, calling George W. Bush to retract his concession

This state's full of sapsucker, hillbilly, and Cajun relatives of mine, and there ain't enough dignity in the bunch of 'em to keep a chigger still long enough to brush his hair.

Huey Long

The kind of thing I'm good at is knowing every politician in the state and remembering where he itches. And I know where to scratch him.

Earl Long

Being governor doesn't mean a thing anymore in this country. We're nothing. Just high-paid ornaments is all. I'm thinking of running for president myself.

George Wallace

He was something like the dark side of the moon of the whole democratic proposition.

> *Marshall Frady, on George Wallace*

God, don't let me die. I have so much to do.

> *Huey Long's last words*

Corruption and Scandal

You get indicted for using your influence to aid drug traffickers. You must pay a fine of $20,000 and lose votes.

> *A card from a board game called Politricks Louisiana: The Political Game*

[I could not lose unless I was] caught in bed with a dead girl or a live boy.

Edwin Edwards, on his campaign for governor of Louisiana

Strange indeed it is that the state that produced Jeffersons and Madisons [not to mention, Washingtons and Lees] should end the millennium led by preachers and fools.

Description of Virginia, in B.C. Hall's and C.T. Wood's
The South

When a politician says, "We've run a clean, honest campaign," he really means, "I spent $30,000 on private detectives and those peckerwoods didn't find a speck of dirt on my opponent."

Lewis Grizzard

Analysis

The demagogues have always understood that Southerners love the grand gesture.

> *Alan Leveritt*

~~~

The one thing that doesn't abide majority rule is a person's conscience.

> *Harper Lee*

~~~

The first words I spoke as a baby were *Mommy, Daddy,* and *constituency.*

> *Pat Robertson, on growing up in a prominent Virginia political family*

~~~

A riot is the language of the unheard.

> *Martin Luther King Jr.*

That bunch up there [in Washington] is so divided that it's like a bunch of bullfrogs with no brains just hoppin' around one another tryin' to find a place to sit down.

Rev. Howard Finster

Americans as a rule think everything can be fixed, but I don't think that.

Doris Betts

All the way from styles in head-gear to opinions on the tariff, the flavor and the color of things in Washington are Southern.

Judson C. Welliver, on politics in America after the election of Woodrow Wilson

Southern Sports

Sports is like war without the killing.

Ted Turner

Fans

I can tell you in just a heartbeat what my fascination with sports is. It's this: I think all of us are looking for that which does not admit of bullshit. You can't get it in a marriage, you can't get it in a—to use a word I hate—relationship, you can't get it from the church or the government.

Harry Crews

A wrestling fan is not like a football fan. They are more vicious, more sadistic.

Texan wrestler Ox Baker

Tiger Stadium in Baton Rouge on a Saturday night of football is an American phenomenon. All around us, thousands of raucous Cajuns, in from the swamps and canebrakes, were dining on jambalaya and gumbo and étouffée and boiled crawfish. And most of them, of course, had been imbibing brawny substances for twenty-four hours at the least.

Willie Morris

We believe that on the eighth day the Lord created the Crimson Tide.

Alabama Senator Jeremiah Denton

Church-dressed spectators cheering in the stands while large young men beat the hell out of one another.

Diane Roberts, describing an Ole Miss–Alabama football game

Most of the South loves defense. This is because people here are always more interested in stopping forward movement than they are in making any forward movement of their own.

Nanci Kincaid, Balls

Coaches

Few things were important to Tom Landry but Christ, family, and football, and, by golly, that made an impression on us.

Lee Roy Jordan

Tom Landry knew you could pray all you wanted, but if you can't play football, you're gonna get your butt beat on Sunday. Amen.

Walt Garrison

I don't want you to concern yourself with what has happened to me. . . . You need to look forward to playing football next September. I want you guys to do everything you can to bring the Cowboys back to the top of the NFL.

Tom Landry's final words to his players, after being fired as coach of the Dallas Cowboys

I know this much: Alabama football will survive anything, because we play the most interesting football there is—we win.

Bear Bryant

If you don't learn anything but self-discipline, then athletics is worthwhile.

Bear Bryant

One reason why we got what they call *football preeminence* here in the South is that we got a tradition of supervision and discipline. If I want a boy, I can put my hand on him in the dorm. If he's just turned loose in town, no telling where he'll be.

University of Alabama football coach Gene Stallings

If a coach doesn't have strong Alabama connections, then he doesn't belong in Alabama. I call this the *No Yankees need apply* rule.

Nanci Kincaid, Balls

Coach is what you call him.
It's a title, like *God.*

Diane Roberts on University of Alabama football coach Gene Stallings

Football

It is no doubt a cliche, yet true, that Southern football is a religion.

Willie Morris

In the South, football is creatively confused with religion, chivalry, the Civil War, and women.

Diane Roberts

Football is less a way out than a way of life. No other sport has a chance in Alabama.

Paul Hemphill

In Alabama, football is a way of life.

Bear Bryant

Snap. Over his head and out of the endzone for a safety! They've given us two points! Can you believe that? They snapped that ball a hundred miles in a tight spiral and blew it over the punter's head in the back of the endzone and in the hedge—the wounded hedge. Safety!

> *"The Voice of the Georgia Bulldogs" Larry Munson, calling a play that gave Georgia a 15-14 lead over Ole Miss*

If teaching athletes the importance of education ruins the football program, then the football program does not belong in the university.

> *Linda Bensel-Meyers, associate professor of English at the University of Tennessee, who alleges academic fraud in the school's athletic department*

He's done more for integration in the South than Martin Luther King did in twenty years.

> *University of Alabama assistant football coach Jerry Claiborne, on Sam Cunningham, a black running back who led the University of Southern California to a 42-21 victory over Alabama, convincing Bear Bryant to recruit more black athletes*

In the South, college football bears the imprint of the Civil War—taking territory and commiting acts of controlled violence for what coaches tell the boys is honor.

Diane Roberts

Go Braves! And take the Falcons with you.

Bumper sticker in Atlanta

The most serious invasion of the North since Lee was stopped at Gettysburg.

A Birmingham sportswriter in 1920, when two Southern college football squads were traveling North to play "Yankee academies"

Golf

I never pray on a golf course. Actually, the Lord answers my prayers everywhere except on the course.

Billy Graham

This was the very golf links, he had reason to believe, where his grandfather had played an exhibition round with the great Bobby Jones in 1925 or thereabouts. It was an ancient sort of links, dating back from the golden age of country clubs, with sturdy rain shelters of green-stained wood and old-fashioned ball washers on each tee and soft rolling bunkers as peaceful as an old battlefield.

Walker Percy, The Last Gentleman

Whoa! Mama, stay up.

Bill Clinton to his ball after teeing off

Some golf shots I wouldn't trade for an orgasm.

Willie Nelson

At Augusta, history is the biggest thing. . . . It's got more to do with history and green jackets and azaleas than playing the course.

Bib Ritekka, on the Masters

I hear you lost your swing. I guess we got to find it.

Steven Pressfield, The Legend of Bagger Vance

If you don't get goosebumps when you walk into this place, you don't have a pulse.

Hal Sutton, on the Augusta National golf course

There is nothing so demoralizing as missing a short putt.

Bobby Jones

Golf . . . is usually played with the outward appearance of great dignity. It is, nevertheless, a game of considerable passion, either of the explosive type, or that which burns inwardly and sears the soul.

Bobby Jones

If I needed advice from my caddie, he'd be hitting the shots and I'd be carrying the bag.

Bobby Jones

Huntin' and Fishin'

The only way to make hunting a sport is to give the animals guns so they can shoot back.

Lewis Grizzard

There is no escaping the conviction that fishing in the South is pursued for its own sake, and not as a means of recuperation between business deals.

Clarence Cason

What's so great about fly fishing is that it allows men to exercise their fascination for gadgetry while giving the appearance of nature-loving, sensitive primitivists.

Alan Jacobs

In just a moment I got a strike as solid as a blow on the shoulder. I took my time and pulled out a black-filigreed brook trout about nine inches long. I disengaged the hook and knocked his head on a rock. I broke off a forky twig slipped it through his mouth and gill, and stuck the twig deep into the bank so he could dangle in the water and keep fresh.

Fred Chappell, I Am One of You Forever

What tickled me was how he'd set the hook. He'd lean way back when a fish hit, and you'd think he was going to fall out of the boat, but then the fish would be hooked and Charlie's arm would be cranking on the reel and he'd tow it in.

Larry Brown

Ten is the age when boys should start hunting. Girls won't have anything to do with them and they can't drink whiskey.

Vic Miller

The thing I always liked best about hunting was the moment when the animal wandered into my gun sights and didn't know I was there. It was like being invisible, like leaving my familiar self and becoming a different person.

Tony Earley

No matter what any woman tells you, hunting puts a man back in touch with his blood. Your mother may think killing is cruel or superfluous now that food comes wrapped in cellophane, but a man has to keep his killer instincts honed, else he loses his humanity.

Vic Miller

Other Sports

There are things that are beyond human control ... and that's what makes the real winners over the people that just win a few races.

Richard Petty

~~~

You mean that Louisville, Kentucky, is not the home of all great ocean rowers? Well, before that, I was the first woman to ski to the South Pole, and there aren't many polar explorers from Kentucky either.

> *Tori Murden, the first woman and the first American to row solo across the Atlantic Ocean, on being asked what drew a Kentuckian to the ocean*

~~~

I tried to enhance the game itself. I tried to be the best basketball player I could be.

Michael Jordan

Everybody liked Junior so much. He was driving for all of us. He was the best. Junior was just a good, ol' boy.

Joyce Wilburn, fan of racing hero Junior Johnson

There is something about jumping a horse over a fence, something that makes you feel good. Perhaps it's the risk, the gamble. In any event, it's a thing I need.

William Faulkner

Getting away with cheating was easy. It was based on how smart you were. But you really didn't have to be that smart because the officials sure weren't smart at all.

North Carolina racing legend Junior Johnson

Southern History

As one beleaguered historian has observed, the central theme of Southern history is a search for the central theme. It has been about as elusive as the Unpardonable Sin.

Fred Hobson

The Civil War

I can anticipate no greater calamity for the country than a dissolution of the Union. It would be an accumulation of all the evils we complain of, and I am willing to sacrifice anything but honor for its preservation.

Robert E. Lee

Damn the torpedoes, full speed ahead.

Union Admiral David Farragut

Can there ever be any thorough national fusion of the
Northern and Southern states? I think not. In fact, the
Union will be shaken almost to dislocation whenever a very
serious question between the states arises.

Samuel Taylor Coleridge

**I believe, myself, that the Civil War was about
slavery. People who say it wasn't are like people
who say that the impeachment of Bill Clinton
was not about sex.**

Roy Blount Jr.

My family lived on rats during the Siege
of Vicksburg. And we've never gotten
over it.

*Overheard at a recent Southern Festival of Books in Nashville,
after a speaker had urged Southerners to get over the Civil War*

It was . . . through a movie that I learned the sad truth that the South had, in fact, not won the Civil War, contrary to what I'd been told both at home and at school.

John Grisham, A Painted House

To give things labels, we may say that the [Civil] War gave the South the Great Alibi and gave the North the Treasury of Virtue.

Robert Penn Warren

Now the chandelier hung dark. It was twisted askew and most of the prisms were broken, as if the Yankee occupants had made their beauty a target for their boots.

Margaret Mitchell, Gone With the Wind

Then the North and the South fought, and the consequences were disastrous to both.

John Crowe Ransom

The remark has been made that in the Civil War the North reaped the victory and the South the glory.

Richard Weaver

The Civil War is our *Iliad*

Shelby Foote

For every Southern boy fourteen years old, not once but whenever he wants it, there is the instant where it's still not yet two o'clock on that July afternoon in 1863, the brigades are in position behind the rail fence, the guns are laid and ready in the woods and the furled flags are already loosed to break out.

William Faulkner

In the South, the war is what A.D. is elsewhere.

Mark Twain

The pain of the Confederate Memorial is very great; the defeat it speaks of is complete. Defeat like this leads to religion.

V. S. Naipaul

I think it's important that the boys from the South should be remembered.

William F. Chaney, on outbidding the National Park Service for the Antietam Battlefield in Virginia, where he has created a Civil War museum and gift shop

From the helicopter the father uses to re-seed the forests further south, you can still see Sherman's March to the Sea, the old burnage in new growth trees, the bright cities that have sprung from the towns the drunken Federal troops torched.

Mark Richard

It's fortunate that war is so terrible, or else we should love it too much.

Robert E. Lee

After the Civil War

For Southerners born of my generation and later, the defining moment in our region's history was not the Civil War but the Civil Rights Movement.

John T. Edge

Country people were not impoverished. They were simply poor.

Will D. Campbell, from his memoir of growing up in Depression-era Mississippi

She told me that the best she could do these days was to give hobos a room in exchange for chopping wood, and how she had to cook rabbits and make coffee out of roasted sweet potatoes.

Lee Smith, on the Depression South, in Oral History

I mean no disrespect, but isn't that war over?

South Carolina congressman Todd Rutherford, on a proposal to raise the Confederate flag to mark the anniversary of the day South Carolina became the first state to secede from the Union

"You'll hear folks say hell, it don't hardly make no difference"—she referred to the Depression which she had already characterized as "old Hoover's fault"—"and for them in the hollers it's true, I reckon, you know how things was up there all along . . . but down here in town it's another story."

Lee Smith, Oral History

All that Depression wasn't paid too much attention to. We just managed and went through it.

Onnie Lee Logan, on Alabama during the Depression

World War II changed the South more deeply than any event since the Civil War.

The Oxford Book of the American South

The Past and Memory

The past and the present coexist here as nowhere on earth, side by side, as though one cannot live without the other.

Eddy L. Harris

~~~

The past is never dead. It's not even past.

Gavin Stevens, in William Faulkner's Requiem for a Nun

~~~

I come from the flat country east of Raleigh in North Carolina, a peculiar part of the world that even today seems to exist about twenty years in the past.

Jim Grimsley

When an old man dies, a library burns to the ground.

Bill Ferris

As he hears his own lips parroting the sad clichés of 1850 does the Southerner sometimes wonder if the words are his own? Does he ever, for a moment, feel the desperation of being caught in some great Time-machine, like a treadmill, and doomed to an eternal effort without progress?

Robert Penn Warren

The past should be magnified in order to keep the present in its place.

Allen Tate

It's only in the South that the past is a cause, an industry and institution, a constant companion who's not always soft-spoken and discreet.

Hal Crowther

It is well to remember that the past, though having meaning, cannot serve as an objective for contemporary man.

Jean Toomer, Essentials

My past seems a fine gray like good old movie rain.

Barry Hannah

It's a deeply humbling experience to come back to the place where it all started . . . and think about how far you've come.

Oprah Winfrey, on returning to her home town of Kosciusko, Mississippi

Time rushes toward us with its hospital tray of infinitely varied narcotics, even while it is preparing us for its inevitably fatal operation.

Tennessee Williams, The Rose Tattoo

One can hardly hail from two more historically losing causes than the South and Judaism. Both my cultures have long, tragic pasts, and not one jot of it has been forgotten.

Mississippi author Edward Cohen

In the South, perhaps more than any other region, we go back to our home in dreams and memories, hoping it remains what it was on a lazy, still summer's day twenty years ago.

Willie Morris

In many ways [the South] has actually always marched away, as to this day it continues to do, from the present toward the past.

W. J. Cash, The Mind of the South

History in Society

Even the most romantic and brutal of us are well aware of the blood price that somebody (maybe not us, but somebody) has to pay for the magnolia-scented arcadia.

Donna Tartt

The current generation of undergraduates, so often indicted by their teachers and even their parents for apathy and avarice, should be encouraged in nearly any form of activism or idealism they embrace. Their hearts are in the right place, even if their discovery that racists helped to build their university is like kids in Lapland discovering the snow.

Hal Crowther

Beware of those who speak of the spiral of history; they are preparing a boomerang. Keep a steel helmet ready.

Ralph Ellison

In all of us there is a hunger, marrow-deep, to know our heritage, to know who we are and where we have come from. Without this enriching knowledge, there is a hollow yearning. No matter what our attainments in life, there is still a vacuum, an emptiness, and the most disquieting loneliness.

Alex Haley

What I have learned from my long affair with Mississippi is that America's greatest strength, and its greatest weakness, is our belief that we can always start over, that things can be made better, transcended.

Anthony Walton

Even now, any common lyncher becomes a defender of the Southern tradition, and any rabble-rouser the gallant leader of a thin gray line of heroes, his hat on saber-point to provide reference by which to hold formation in the charge.

Robert Penn Warren

Scarlett hated them, these smiling, light-footed strangers, these proud fools who took pride in something they had lost, seeming to be proud that they had lost it.

> *Margaret Mitchell,* Gone With the Wind

We are not the makers of history.
We are made by history.

> *Martin Luther King Jr.*

The South is the region that history has happened to.

> *Richard Weaver*

And the nigga done read history
yet his eyes didn't see
the only reason you a nigga cause somebody else
want you to be.

> *Cee-Lo, of Atlanta rap group Goodie Mob*

The Language of the South

In the South, [conversation] is moonshine passed slowly to all who care to lift the bottle.

Roy Reed

Talk About Talking

Southerners think words are like people. Peculiar people. Mix a bunch of them together and you can't tell what might happen.

Roy Blount Jr.

I think the Southerner is a talker by nature, but not only a talker—we are used to an audience.

Eudora Welty

I'm always asked why I write about women, and I end up saying it's because I grew up around a lot of women who talked and a lot of men who didn't talk much.

Clyde Edgerton

In Southern English, "naked" means you ain't got no clothes on, while "nekkid" means you ain't got no clothes on and you're up to something.

Lewis Grizzard

We wrestle with our words the way we do with our children, so as to get syncopated with them.

Roy Blount Jr.

Quite early, any Southerner with a literary turn begins to realize that the language around him is radioactive.

Guy Davenport

An extremely wise friend of mine from Louisiana once observed that Southerners can explain almost everything that is wrong with their bodies, as well as various machinery and appliances, with the phrases "backed up," "shorted out," or "blew out." These usually will be followed by the words "on him" As in, "You know his engine just blew out on him."

Julia Reed

We will chew on our choice of words, engage in dialogue with our words, roll them around in our mouth, enjoy them for the peculiar artifacts or organisms that they are.

Roy Blount Jr.

Language strikes me as a miracle, a thing the deepest mind adores.

Barry Hannah

The Southern Accent

A Southerner talks music.

Mark Twain

~~~

His Tennessee accent (bleached out by St. Albans prep and the Ivy League) loped back in like a long-lost dog.

Diane Roberts, referring to Al Gore's speech to the NAACP

~~~

Come January we are going to have a president in the White House who doesn't speak with an accent.

Jimmy Carter

~~~

I wanted to smell that Louisiana earth, feel that Louisiana sun. . . . hear that Louisiana dialect. . . . There's no more beautiful sound anywhere.

Ernest Gaines

They say Louisiana is somewhat like a banana republic, say Guatemala. That's not true. They speak better English in Guatemala.

Jack Kneece

Strangers told us we spoke Elizabethan English, that we were contemporary ancestors to everyone else. They told us the correct way to pronounce *Appalachia,* as if we didn't know where we'd been living for the past three hundred years.

Chris Offutt, on linguistics doctoral students visiting his Haldeman, Kentucky, hometown, in The Same River Twice: A Memoir

The educated Southerner has no use for an *r,* except at the beginning of a word.

Mark Twain

Southerners can probably say "shit" better than anybody else. We give it the ol' two-syllable "shee-yet," which strings it out a bit and gives it more ambience, if words can have ambience.

Lewis Grizzard

Memphians don't speak English, they speak Memphish.

Ed Weathers

Vic [Chesnutt] has somehow turned *pronunciation* into an instrument. He's constantly resurrecting and warping syllables that we have, through habit or sloth, nearly elided into oblivion.

John J. Sullivan, on the Athens, Georgia, singer

Southern Lit

I write out of a greed for lives and language. A need to listen to the orchestra of living.

Barry Hannah

What Is It About the South?

It takes a story to make a story.

Flannery O'Connor

~~~~~

Per capita, the South doesn't produce all that many writers, any more than kangaroos amount to a great percentage of prizefighters. It's just that you can tell right away which prizefighters are kangaroos.

Roy Blount Jr.

Why has the South produced so many good writers?
Because we got beat.

> *Walker Percy*

You've got to come from somewhere. Not everyone
can be born in the Museum of Modern Art.

> *Fred Chappell*

With Mississippi, many South-watchers have
pondered . . . how that state, more than once labeled
"The Heart of Darkness," and accustomed to
finishing dead last in nearly all cultures indexes by
which H. L. Mencken measured civilization, could
produce Faulkner, the greatest writer the English-
speaking world has seen this century, as well as
enough other superb writers as to top any other
state in the South, and perhaps the nation.

> *Fred Hobson*

179
SOUTHERN
LIT

In most of America, probably because of television, stories are drying up. Not in New Orleans. They grow in abundance here, like the flowering vines, and the myrtles, the bananas, and the figs.

> *Andrei Codrescu, "The Muse Is Always Half-Dressed in New Orleans"*

Southern Writers, Southern Writing

My mother, Southern to the bone, once told me, "All Southern literature can be summed up in these words: 'On the night the hogs ate Willie, Mama died when she heard what Daddy did to Sister.'" She raised me up to be a Southern writer, but it wasn't easy.

Pat Conroy

I don't like Southern writing; all the novels seem to be about three generations of women who sit on the porch and talk for 400 pages.

Florence King

I am often asked if I consider myself a Southern writer, and, to be honest, my answer depends on . . . whether or not my questioner smiles when he calls me that.

Tony Earley

It doesn't bother me at all to be called a Southern writer. It is the job of any writer to create a vision that is unique, and if you are successful in that you should be satisfied. I don't see why people wouldn't be proud to be a Southern anything.

Scott Morris

There is no such thing as Southern writing or Southern literature or Southern ethos.

Richard Ford

The day of regional Southern writing is all gone. I think that people who try to write in that style are usually repeating a phased-out genre or doing Faulkner badly.

Walker Percy

Among certain Southern writers there's been a kind of competition to determine who was raised roughest of all.

Hal Crowther

I am a writer, and a Southerner, but not a Southern writer.

Guy Davenport

Great writers are exiles, either spiritually or geographically.

Literary critic Louis Rubin

Whenever I'm asked why Southern writers particularly have a penchant for writing about freaks, I say it is because we are still able to recognize one.

Flannery O'Connor

Well, in the South they like you dead or away.

Barry Hannah

You didn't try to pass it off as truth, did you?

Harry Crews's mother, on hearing he sold his first novel

Anytime a contemporary Southern writer hears someone call their work gothic, they know they are only moments away from being compared unfavorably to Faulkner and O'Connor, and then being asked to get on with their lives.

Tony Earley

Garrulous and melodious, their voices shift effortlessly
between the King James version of the Bible and the old
liar pontificating in front of the kerosene stove.

Tom Payne, on certain Southern writers

All literature is gossip.

Truman Capote

**All my stories are about the action of grace on a
character who is not very willing to support it,
but most people think of these stories as hard,
hopeless, and brutal.**

Flannery O'Connor

The authors contributing to this book are Southerners, well
aquainted with one another and of similar tastes, though
not necessarily living in the same physical community, and
perhaps only at this moment aware of themselves as a single
group of men.

From the introduction to I'll Take My Stand: The
South and the Agrarian Tradition

Why Write?

Whatever our theme in writing, it is old and tried.
Whatever our place, it has been visited by the stranger, it
will never be new again. It is only the vision that can be
new; but that is enough.

Eudora Welty

Being a fiction writer is a good way to go
crazy, it's a good way to be a nervous
wreck, it's a good way to become a
drunk.

Harry Crews

It's an illusion that writers have a lot of choice about what
they write. Your stories are your stories. They're the only
ones you can really tell, and if you try telling ones the
world would like you tell, you'll do it badly.

Dorothy Allison

I use language to order my past. I feel like if I can get all of that in order, then I have a network for the future and everything will be okay.

Kaye Gibbons

Writing is a way for me of discovering what I think about something. I think that's the great delight in writing.

Peter Taylor

Really the writer doesn't want success . . . He knows he has a short span of life, that the day will come when he must pass through the wall of oblivion, and he wants to leave a scratch on that wall—Kilroy was here—that somebody a hundred, or a thousand years later will see.

William Faulkner

Anybody who has survived his childhood has enough information to last him the rest of his days.

Flannery O'Connor

It costs so much to write a decent sentence.

Maya Angelou

In a materialistic and secular world, language and literature, and the richness of language is literature, seems to me as the best if not the only way to rescue us from the rapid advance of a confusion of tongues.

Andrew Lytle

Poetry is the kind of knowledge by which we must know that which we cannot know otherwise.

John Crowe Ransom

187
SOUTHERN
LIT

Since where we lived and how we lived was almost
hermetically sealed from everybody else, fabrication became
a way of life. Making up stories, it seems to me now, was
not only a way for us to understand the way we lived but
also a defense against it.

Harry Crews

Writers on Writers

A practical jokester, a foe of injustice, a friend to all dogs; a
man who loved taverns, and old cemeteries, who poured big
old slugs of bourbon into his coffee to warm himself up
on chilly autumn nights.

Donna Tartt describing Willie Morris

**Truman Capote had a lovely, poetic ear. He did
not have a good mind.**

Norman Mailer

Everywhere I go I'm asked if I think the university stifles writers. My opinion is that they don't stifle enough of them. There's many a bestseller that could have been prevented by a good teacher.

Flannery O'Connor

If the South has a Chekhov, he is Peter Taylor.

Allen Tate

Each morning he would get up at dawn and swim, and then from six a.m. to noon he would work in his little office, a converted pool house. He would always write, whether letters or journals or plays. It was his great joy, his appetite.

Robert Falls, on Tennessee Williams

Cormac McCarthy at his best—McCarthy writing with the throttle wide open—is still the closest thing to heroin you can buy in a bookstore.

Hal Crowther

Books

It captures all the awe and strangeness of being a boy in the South. It seems part tall-tale, front-porch reminiscence, ghost story and family saga—all the stuff the South does better than anyone else.

Pat Conroy, on Wayne Greenhaw's A Remembrance

If you don't like my book, write your own. If you don't think you can write a novel, that ought to tell you something.

Rita Mae Brown

Finishing a book is just like you took a child out in the yard and shot it.

Truman Capote

I love being in the same paragraph as Margaret Mitchell. In literary circles, you're not supposed to say that. But you could argue, and I would if anyone would listen, that *Gone With the Wind* is the greatest American novel ever written.

Tom Wolfe

I read the same books over and over. It gets to where I read not only because I love the book itself, but because I love the memory of all the other times I've read it.

Bailey White

It's like reading *Madame Bovary* while listening to Loretta Lynn and watching *Guiding Light*.

Roy Blount Jr., describing Lee Smith's novel Black Mountain Breakdown

Until I feared I would lose it, I never loved to read. One does not love breathing.

Harper Lee, To Kill a Mockingbird

There have been too many [books] in which some young man is looking forward, backward or sideways in anger. Or in which some Southern youth is being chased through the magnolia bushes by his aunt. She catches him on page twenty-eight with horrid results.

Bennett Cerf

William Faulkner

I discovered Faulkner at a late age—thank God.

Padgett Powell

INTERVIEWER: Some people say they can't understand your writing, even after they read it two or three times. What approach would you suggest for them?
WILLIAM FAULKNER: Read it four times.

From William Faulkner: Three Decades of Criticism

If a writer has to rob his mother, he will not hesitate; the "Ode on a Grecian Urn" is worth any number of old ladies.

William Faulkner

I love Virginians because Virginians are all such snobs and I like snobs. A snob has to spend so much time being a snob that he has little time left to meddle with you.

William Faulkner

No one wants his mule and wagon stalled on the same track the *Dixie Limited* is roaring down.

Flannery O'Connor, referring to William Faulkner

The aim of every artist is to arrest motion, which is life, by artificial means and hold it fixed so that a hundred years later, when a stranger looks at it, it moves again since it is life.

William Faulkner

People need trouble—a little frustration to sharpen the spirit on, toughen it. Artists do; I don't mean you need to live in a rat hole or gutter, but you have to learn fortitude, endurance. Only vegetables are happy.

William Faulkner

Faulkner has become a kind of factory up here. . . . It is something that I think he would have resented, although he probably would have had a good time for a while.

Barry Hannah, on Oxford, Mississippi

Perhaps it's true that Faulkner, if he had been born in, say, Pasadena, might very well still have had that universal quality of mind, but instead of writing *Light in August* he would have gone into television or written universal ads for Jantzen bathing suits.

William Styron

One of the tritest and most tedious
examples of a trite and tedious genre.

Vladimir Nabokov, describing Faulkner's Light in August

I could not see the writing as having come from a boy
named Bill—I saw the shelf of books in the library as
having sprung full-blown if not from the hip of Zeus then
at least from the head of a non-mortal.

Padgett Powell

**Like many Mississippians, I shied away from
Faulkner, who was at once remote and right
there in your own backyard, the powerful
resident alien.**

Barry Hannah

Living in the South, we are all post-
Faulknerians.

Diane Roberts

Southern Humor

Being humorous in the South is like being motorized in Los Angeles or argumentative in New York—humorous is not generally a whole calling in and of itself, it's just something that you're in trouble if you aren't.

Roy Blount Jr.

Funny Stuff

A joke going around down here asks why Southern women don't like group sex. Give up? Too many thank-you notes.

John Shelton Reed

Storytelling and copulation are the two chief forms of amusement in the South. They're inexpensive and easy to procure.

Robert Penn Warren

~~~

If I am in luck, the next question is, "Do Southerners laugh at different things than Northerners do?" "Yes," I say. "Northerners."

Roy Blount Jr., on book tour interviews

~~~

About like when *anybody* shoots at you.

Bill Clinton's mother, on being asked how it felt when one of her husbands shot at her

~~~

The South may not always be right, but by God it's never wrong!

Brother Dave Gardner

I've never been jealous. Not even when my dad finished the fifth grade a year before I did.

Jeff Foxworthy

I don't hate Yankees, but I have a friend who does. His hobby is reading the obituary page of *The New York Times*.

Lewis Grizzard

Where did indoor plants live before we built houses for them?

Atlanta Journal-Constitution *columnist Ron Hudspeth*

[My granddaddy] said folks who ain't got nothing to brag about except their ancestors are like potatoes—the best part of 'em is buried.

Ludlow Porch

If you ever start feeling like you have the goofiest, craziest, most dysfunctional family in the world, all you have to do is go to a state fair. Because five minutes at the fair, you'll be going, "You know, we're alright. We are dang near royalty."

Jeff Foxworthy

Vagrancy used to be an actual charge, before Marlon Brando and others made it into a national pastime.

Barry Hannah

South Carolina is too small for a republic and too large for a lunatic asylum.

J. L. Petigru

If I only had a little humility, I would be perfect.

Ted Turner

I'm about as tall as a shotgun, and just as noisy.

Truman Capote

I happen to know quite a bit about the South. Spent twenty years there one night.

Dick Gregory

Once when I was golfing in Georgia I hooked the ball into a swamp. I went in after it and found an alligator wearing a shirt with a picture of a little golfer on it.

Buddy Hackett

He's so slow that he takes an hour and a half to watch *60 Minutes*.

Edwin Edwards, on his Republican opponent in the race for governor of Louisiana

Sometimes when I look at my children, I say to myself, "Lillian, you should have stayed a virgin."

Lillian Carter, mother of Jimmy Carter

I don't deserve any credit for turning the other cheek as my tongue is always in it.

Flannery O'Connor

That town was so backward, even the Episcopalians handled snakes.

Doug Marlette

"Do you believe in infant baptism?" one old boy asks another, who replies, "Believe in it? Hell, I've seen it done."

Roy Blount Jr.

Talk About Humor

I don't tell funny stories, I tell stories funny.

Jerry Clower

I am convinced there is only one place where there is no laughter . . . and that's hell.

Jerry Clower

If you want to, you can say that Southern humor deals with "typical" concerns of the region: dirt, chickens, defeat, family, religion, prejudice, collard greens, politics, and diddie wah diddie. But are not these concerns, boiled down, pretty much like everybody else's?

Roy Blount Jr.

The Southern humorists who put me off are those who rest their crabby/maudlin appeal upon the assumption that certain of their characters (for instance, themselves) are just about the most precious *thangs*.

Roy Blount Jr.

Southern
Music

You've got to have smelled a lot of mule manure before you can sing like a hillbilly.

Hank Williams

Music and Life

I guess everybody enjoys their life. But being able to play music has added to mine. My life as an ordinary citizen has been good. But if you add the music, it doubles it.

Luderin Darbone of the Hackberry Ramblers

You don't know, man, I done lived a life, wasn't no happiness in it. The only thing I got a thrill out of was playing music.

Blues and swing musician Dave Myers

No matter how high tech we get, people are still getting divorced somewhere today. Somebody just lost a loved one that they're grieving over. Somebody just lost his job down at the factory. Some ol' boy's laid out drunk all night. And some ol' boy went out last night with another woman, not his wife. . . . It hasn't changed since the beginning of time. I can still write about it, and guess what? There's a guy or woman out there that can relate to it, if I write it right.

Nashville songwriter Larry Shell

Music in the South was often a means of making something beautiful out of hardship and misery.

Nicholas Dawidoff

When he isn't laughing, his face manifests an inscrutable weariness. The face of a sixty-four-year-old man who started drinking heavily at eight years of age. A man whose first wife left him, it is said, because he never came home. A man who still drives the back roads of Marshall County with a jar of "battery juice" and a .357 Magnum between his legs.

Jonathan Miles, describing bluesman Junior Kimbrough

In the dark your troubles can fade and you listen to the music and move your feet, knowing it'll take the hurt away, cure whatever ails you.

Larry Brown, in the liner notes to Junior Kimbrough's album, Sad Days, Lonely Nights

I was born with music in me.

Ray Charles

205
SOUTHERN
MUSIC

Billie Joe McAllister and the narrator walked out on that old bridge, and what they ceremoniously dropped into the muddy water below was our innocence. It was a neat little package, but we were too young and too busy to notice.

Ron Carlson, on Bobbie Gentry's "Ode to Billie Joe"

I was a member of a family of sixteen. . . . When we got done with the cotton chopping in the afternoon and dinner in the evening, we'd get together in the yard and start singing church songs. The moon would be shining bright, and the echo would ring out across the fields.

"Pops" Staples of the Staple Singers, recalling his childhood in Mississippi

God comes along every once in a while and puts His hand on people, and He says, "Okay, you'll be the Carter Family. Okay, you'll be Elvis Presley. Okay, you'll be Johnny Cash, and you'll be Hank Williams." But he doesn't say that very often.

June Carter Cash

As he talked . . . he kept reaching out every now and then to touch the guitar. But only as you stroke your pet or touch a charm, or as you finger a weapon or your favorite piece of sports equipment.

Albert Murray

Music in Society

The background music for a two-block beer commercial.

Jonathan Miles, describing the blues music found on Memphis's Beale Street

Even as Southern music grew in popularity, the music industry tamed its spontaneity, bled its interracial message, consumed its profits, and commodified its style. Like stock car racing, rock 'n' roll became diluted for mass consumption.

Pete Daniel

I'm always trying to look beyond the South—although sometimes I look at the South with a microscope.

Athens, Georgia, songwriter Vic Chesnutt

I wonder how much the City of New Orleans charges for selling out its own priceless and irreplaceable cultural heritage.

Tom Piazza, on a New Orleans crackdown on street musicians

I got piles of magazine articles on me. You can't eat that. You know what? It don't taste too good.

Rockabilly legend Charlie Feathers

All Southern music is a tangle of crossed lines, shared sources, and interweaving destinies.

Tom Piazza

I'm certainly not a professional Southerner. There's much about the South I detest. Like most Southerners, I love it and hate it at the same time.

Carlisle Floyd, composer of the operas Susannah, Willie Stark, *and* Cold Sassy Tree

We shall be fortunate if "Dixie" does not impose its very name on our country.

Anonymous, 1861, referring to the song

Hip hop has given us a closer and clearer definition of ourselves and our lives. I pray we realize what a blessing we have in music and discontinue the disrespect and separatism that's killing us literally and killing the minds and souls of the children who want to be like us.

Cee-Lo, of Atlanta rap group Goodie Mob

The Blues

Anybody singing the blues is in a deep pit yelling for help.

Mahalia Jackson

The blues offers an implicit, comprehensive, existential philosophy that operates outside the framework of Christian belief, but is haunted by it just the same; they are the Delta's spiritual poles—one sacred and the other profane.

Tom Piazza

I try to say something people, something just to pacify,
I try to say something people, something just to pacify.
I might not have lived right all of my life, but people please
believe me I've tried.

B. B. King, "Why I Sing the Blues"

My room was empty, and my woman was gone,
My room was empty, and my woman was gone,
I didn't have a nickel, and all my clothes in
pawn.

Memphis Slim, "Empty Room Blues"

Bluesmen, history tells us, rarely retire.

Jonathan Miles

When I started off at those house parties, I never felt that
I'd be going to no festivals or things then 'cause I was kind
of ashamed. But once I started out, got the bashful out of
me, I had it made.

Bluesman R. L. Burnside

Junior Kimbrough is the beginning and the end of music. Ain't no one can play like him. No one. There is no greater sound than Junior's cottonpatch blues.

Rockabilly legend Charlie Feathers

Through the smoke and the racket of the noisy Chicago bar float Louisiana bayous, muddy old swamps, Mississippi dust and sun, cotton fields, lonesome roads, train whistles in the night, mosquitoes at dawn, and the Rural Free Delivery that never brings the right letter.

Langston Hughes

Ain't nobody in the world ever been able to holler "Hey Bo Weevil" like her. Not like Ma Rainey.

Anonymous

The Delta's relative prosperity elevated the blues to an act of commerce and franchise; the hard dirt of the hills kept the music close to its original folk voice.

> *Jonathan Miles, comparing Delta blues to the blues of the Mississippi hill country*

It's easy to hear the earthiness in most Memphis music; it's sucked up so much richness from the soil, been watered by the sweat of so many hard-living Delta blues artists.

> *Stephanie Zacharek*

For the Memphis kids in the 1950s who would witness the creation of rock and roll—pure Delta blues wasn't necessarily a detached voice on a piece of black vinyl. . . . The mystery of that sound was not "Where?" but "How?"

> *Robert Gordon,* It Came from Memphis

SOUTHERN
MUSIC

Soul and R&B

If I had to tell somebody who had never been to the South, who had never heard of soul music, what it was, I'd just have to tell him that it's music from the heart, from the pulse, from the innermost feeling. That's my soul, that's how I sing. And that's the South.

Al Green

People down here don't let nobody tell them what to do.

Dan Penn, on being asked what about the South made it a hotbed of music in the early days of soul music

This was the devil's music—you didn't listen to it in the average white Southern home. White teenagers like myself were relegated to sneaking around to hear the music.

R&B record promoter Marion Carter, on "race music" in the 1940s and 1950s.

They called it "suggestive music." . . . Lyrics like "Sock it to me, baby, one more time" or "I'm gonna smoke you all night long" made the parents go crazy and left the teenagers wanting to hear more. Plus it had the tempo we liked to dance to.

Harry Driver, on R&B in the Carolinas during segregation

I'm not going to tell you what's missing in American music. I never telegraph my moves.

James Brown

I don't sing a song unless I feel it. The song don't tug at my heart, I pass on it. I have to believe what I'm doing.

Ray Charles

When you hear his voice in just about any song, it sounds like a smile.

Allen Toussaint, on Lee Dorsey

It now seems that the golden era of soul music in Memphis was one of those increasingly rare periods when artistic achievement and popular success were not in opposition.

Stanley Booth

I never wanted to be famous; I only wanted to be great.

Ray Charles

Country

"If I Said You Had a Beautiful Body, Would You Hold It Against Me?"

Song by country music act the Bellamy Brothers

If there's a honky-tonk within a hundred miles of New Orleans, I've played there.

Veteran steel guitarist Harold Cavallero

Watching a Garth Brooks concert [on television] in the Country Music Hall of Fame is like watching an REO Speedwagon concert in the Rock and Roll Hall of Fame.

Mark Smirnoff, editor of The Oxford American

I'm a country songwriter and we write cry-in-your-beer songs. That's what we do. Something that you can slow dance to.

Willie Nelson

Country music was always the folk music of the white Southern working class.

Paul Hemphill

The chief tension in country music has always been the battle between the old and the new.

Bruce Feiler

I like banjo because sometimes I hear ancestors in the strumming. I like the fiddle-like refrain in "Dixie" for the very same reason. But most of all I like square dancing— the interplay between fiddle and caller, the stomping, the swishing of dresses, the strutting, the proud turnings, the laughter.

> *James Alan McPherson, explaining how a black Southerner could like country music*

[The country music star] had to be from humble beginnings, just like the audience.

> *Chet Flippo*

You give me a hit, and I'd tell Music Row to piss up a stump. . . . You give me a hit record, and I'll run for Congress. You give me a hit, and I'll kiss your ass on the Grand Ole Opry stage on Saturday night and get Minnie Pearl to hold your britches.

> *Tom T. Hall, "The Storyteller's Nashville"*

There are hollers used to call hogs, cows, dogs, mules, and errant fieldhands—and one, a hollerer reports, that will stop a running rabbit in its tracks.

Jeff Baker, reviewing the CD Hollerin', *featuring past winners of the National Hollerin' Contest, held in North Carolina*

Don't be a blueprint. Be an original.

Roy Acuff

"You know, it ain't hard to figure out who to fuck to get *on* the Opry," she said. "The hard thing is figuring out who to fuck to get *off*."

Lucille White, long-time country star, in Lee Smith's The Devil's Dream

Somebody interviewing me once asked me, "What's the Nashville sound?" I was stumbling around for an answer and he got out some coins and shook them and he was right.

Chet Atkins

I would venture to say that loudly denouncing Emmylou Harris will get you killed in an establishment that serves liquor south of Delaware.

Steve Earle

The world was one long night, endless Nashvilles,
A jambalaya of women, whiskey, and pills.

Joseph Bolton, "Lines for Hank Williams"

Rock 'n' Roll

Rock 'n' roll is part of a plot to undermine the morals of the youth of our nation. It is sexualistic, unmoralistic, and the best way to bring people of both races together.

Asa Carter, secretary of the North Alabama White Citizens' Council, 1956

So much of rock 'n' roll is geared towards bothering people. We've been through that stage. We like making music people will enjoy.

Cary Hudson, of the band Blue Mountain

Rock & roll was not a marriage of R&B and country & western. That's white publicity. Rock & roll was just white imitation, a white adaptation of Negro rhythms.

Louis Jordan

221
SOUTHERN
MUSIC

We've heard a lot about these boys and if they behave themselves, we'll give them a right-friendly welcome. Memphis is a clean city. We aim to keep it that way. We will not tolerate any real or simulated sex onstage. No, sir. They can be nude if they like. They can spit. They can even vomit. No law against that, but there must be no lewd or indecent behavior.

Vice Squad Lt. Ronald Howell, before the Sex Pistols's 1978 concert in Memphis

What is a love song if it doesn't have a little bit of creepiness and weirdness in it? Everything does.

Michael Stipe, of R.E.M.

A redneck (if not a hillbilly) with poetic and forensic skills sufficient to fling the likes of Neil Young into the dust.

Dave Marsh, on Lynyrd Skynyrd's Ronnie Van Zant

One day, *Bartlett's* will quote [Vic Chesnutt's] worst lines in a misguided gesture meant to certify him as that rare songwriter of whom we stop to say, "You know what? That guy's actually a poet!"

  John J. Sullivan

I never said I was the King of Rock 'n' Roll. I said simply that I'm the best.

  Jerry Lee Lewis

Lyrics

Your lyrics is what really makes your song, where I'm concerned. It's not the music; it's the lyrics.

  Gospel singer Rev. Willie Morganfield

I would've killed myself, but it made no sense— Commitin' suicide in self-defense.

  Jimmy Dale Gilmore

I taught that weeping willow
how to cry, cry, cry.
I taught the clouds
How to cover up a clear blue sky.

Johnny Cash

Old legs built like barrels,
Wide in the middle, jump start,
Slamming the straddle.

Bull Moose Jackson, from "Bow Legged Woman Just Fine,"
an early R&B song

Devil went down to Georgia, and he was
looking for a soul to steal.

Charlie Daniels Band, "The Devil Went Down to Georgia"

I bought my mind and soul on the river.
I bought my heart in Nashville, Tennessee.

Olu Dara, "Natchez Shopping Blues"

My hair's still curly and my eyes are still blue.
Why don't you love me like you used to do?

Hank Williams

I kinda like the idea of people with one hand cupped to
their ear and going, "What's that they're saying?"

Peter Buck, of R.E.M.

Elvis

I don't know anything about music. In my line, you
don't have to.

Elvis

I don't sound like nobody.

Elvis, on being asked what his music sounded like

[He] shakes his pelvis like any striptease babe in town.

Newspaper columnist Herb Rollins

It was like he came along and whispered some dream in everybody's ear. And somehow we all dreamed it.

> *Bruce Springsteen*

Elvis was a hero to most,
But he never meant shit to me.

> *Public Enemy, "Fight the Power"*

Even though other singers would have come up with a white version of the new black music acceptable to teenage America, of all who did emerge in Elvis's wake none sang as powerfully, or with more than a touch of his magic.

> *Greil Marcus,* Mystery Train

Well, it gets hard sometimes. I have to stop and rest it—but it just automatically wiggles like that.

> *Elvis, on being asked how he kept his leg shaking at the right tempo while he was singing*

I don't believe I'd sing the way I do if God hadn't
wanted me to. My voice is God's will, not mine.

Elvis

I'm grateful. Only I'm afraid. I'm afraid I'll go out like
a light, just like I came on.

Elvis, on his new-found fame, in a 1956 interview

After Elvis it became harder to say that decent people
don't think or say or do certain things.

Charles Taylor

The freedom he brought with him was the
fundamentally American freedom to light out for the
territories, to create your own identity, to eclipse (if
not erase) the boundaries of class and race and still,
to insist that you were part of America.

Charles Taylor

It suggests Elvis as an icon of everyday life. You could—
if you wished—eat a piece of the great man's head.

*Charles Reagan Wilson, on his gelatin mold shaped like
a bust of Elvis*

Like most normal Americans, I prefer the Elvis that
lit up the '50s to the one that flamed out in the
seventies. I see the boy as something like Coca-Cola,
another Southern product that taught the world to
sing but lost its regional flavor in the process.

John Shelton Reed

Somewhere between a demigod and a bat.

*Peter Guralnick, describing the caped Elvis, when he
ended his shows with his arms outstretched*

Tupelo, Mississippi, is the Bethlehem of the South.

Diane Roberts, on Elvis's natal town

Remember, this is a devotional service and if any of you are thinking about laughing or cutting up, I wouldn't if I were you. The others would tear you to pieces before we could get to you.

> *The master of ceremonies at the Elvis Candlelight Vigil, Graceland*

The mother is beaming with pride at what she has caused her son to be doing: imitating Elvis Presley, a form of child abuse not yet recognized by the authorities.

> *John Fergus Ryan, regarding a nine-year-old Elvis impersonator spotted at Graceland during Elvis Week*

He was like a mirror. Whatever you were looking for, you were going to find in him.

> *Marion Keisker, Sam Phillips's assistant at Sun Records*

Art in the South

The obsession with place, with family, with both the personal and the social past; the susceptibility to myth; the love of this light, which is all our own; and the readiness to experiment with dosages of romance that would be fatal to most late-twentieth-century artists.

> *Photographer Sally Mann, listing the ways she describes herself as a Southern artist*

I don't think they knew what they were talking about. I really don't. I think they wrote that because they thought it sounded good.

> *Photographer William Eggleston, on being called "a Southerner through and through" in* The New York Times, *and "strongly identifying with the antebellum South" in* Art in America

We do not have a tradition of image-making that even pretends to compete with our storytelling tradition.

Tom Payne

~~~

I had to find my own way, and Louisiana has been perfect for that. It's almost virgin country for a modern landscape painter, and it's full of people who care about the unique qualities of the place.

Australian-born painter Simon Gunning, on why he moved to New Orleans

~~~

I paint out of the tradition of the blues, of call and recall.

Charlotte, North Carolina, painter Romare Bearden.

~~~

I don't ask nobody to go by my visions. All I can do is tell them the visions I have.

Georgia outsider artist Rev. Howard Finster

Como doesn't normally support things like this, but we're a strange town—when we decide we love certain people and things, we just break our heads doing for it.

Jo Anne Billingsly, on tiny Como, Mississippi's decision to hire an artist-in-residence

I could never be a primitive because fortunately or unfortunately I have had some education and can't be sincerely primitive.

John McCrady

There are painters who depict Southern scenes, but one can only hope that a magnolia or a cotton boll, or even the boll weevil, does not qualify as Southern art.

Tom Payne

I think for a long time I resisted making anything that had anything to do with race simply because it was what was expected.

African American artist Kara Walker

Art depends, in general, like religion, on a right attitude to nature.

> *John Crowe Ransom, from* I'll Take My Stand: The South and the Agrarian Tradition

A cabin on a hill in the region of Mississippi or Louisiana, standing in the open, stained with nature's patina, built from the wood of the surrounding trees, expresses the harmony of architecture and environment that some men spend a lifetime trying to copy.

> *John McCrady*

Have I been vague enough?

> *Painter Todd Murphy, in a 1998 interview*

It's not coincidental that the best visual artist to emerge from Memphis is the photographer William Eggleston, whose m.o. is to find the beautiful in the ugly.

> *Marc Smirnoff*

I haven't had a show in the real South in five years. There have been a few invitations, most noticeably Mississippi. I was invited to show my work as long as there wasn't any sex or violence. I politely declined.

Kara Walker, in a 2000 interview

The poverty can get depressing, but you can't dwell on it. I've been trying to be an artist for ten years. It's a hand-to-mouth existence, full of faith.

Georgia painter Terry Rowlett

At least they will make wonderful ruins.

Senator Thomas P. Gore, on Washington, D.C.'s Roman Revival federal buildings, as quoted by Gore Vidal in "At Home in Washington, D.C."

Eating and Drinking in the South

~~~~~~~~~~~~~~~~~~~~

The only artful way to fix string beans is to cook them almost to death.

Ludlow Porch

Southern Cuisine

Lips are all meat. No gristle, no bone, no nothing. They're bar food, hot and vinegary, great with a beer.

Lionel Dufour to John T. Edge, who was about to sample pig lips for the first time

It was so thick that when you stuck a spoon into it you had a hard time getting it back out, almost as if it were trapped in a pool of quicksand.

> *Steve Yarbrough, describing his grandmother's homemade molasses*

Greens are good for you but it's the drippings that make you want to eat 'em. Taste life!

> *Dexter Weaver,* Automatic Y'all: Weaver D's Guide to the Soul

I'm going back down in New Orleans,
I'm going back down in New Orleans.
Well, I'm going where I can get my rice and beans.

> *Memphis Minnie, "Down in New Orleans"*

Hell, at least I wasn't trying to *hide* the Spam. I had it right out there.

> *Buster Quin to Clyde Edgerton, after his Jamaican Yam and Spam failed to place in a Spam cookoff at a North Carolina state fair*

I'm from Bayou Lafourche, me, so I know all the difference between Cajun *boudin* and New Orleans baloney.

A New Orleans taxi driver, on the local cuisine

Is frying a defining characteristic of the South? A boiled New England dinner eases its way into your system the same way a New England sentence does: without calling much attention to itself. Whereas a dinner of fried panfish (fins and all) and hushpuppies and fried yellow squash says *Hot damn, here I am. I got the grit and I got the grease, come on.*

Roy Blount Jr.

Hot tamales became very much a Delta food. Hell, we were eating them before I ever recall seeing a Mexican.

Shelby Foote

237
EATING
AND
DRINKING
IN
THE
SOUTH

When the taste changes with every bite and the last bite tastes as good as the first, that's Cajun.

Paul Prudhomme

I'll be happy to get home and eat two-year-old ham, corn bread, beaten biscuits, pound cake, yellow-leg fried chicken, and corn pudding.

Kentucky-born food critic Duncan Hines

A fruitcake is much like cooked rice: Each grain must stand alone, and each slice of fruitcake should do the same.

Marie Rudisill, author of Fruitcake: Memories of Truman Capote and Sook

Southern barbecue is the closest thing we have in the U.S. to Europe's wines or cheeses; drive a hundred miles and the barbecue changes.

John Shelton Reed

If you're eating barbecue, you deserve to know exactly what you're getting.

South Carolina State Representative John Snow, on the "Truth in Barbecue" bill

I opened the safe, took a biscuit off a plate, and punched a hole in it with my finger. Then with a jar of cane syrup, I poured the hole full, waited for it to soak in good, and then poured again.

Harry Crews

**Everybody has the right to think whose food is most gorgeous,
And I nominate Georgia's.**

Ogden Nash

239
EATING
AND
DRINKING
IN
THE
SOUTH

The best thing I ever got from their table was possum,
which we *never* got at home because mama would not cook
it. She said she knew it would taste like a wet dog smells.
But it did not. Auntie could cook it in a way that would
break your heart.

> *Harry Crews*

Grits is the first truly American food.

> *Turner Catledge*

**If you are what you eat, a visit to North
Carolina could make you a very interesting
person.**

> *North Carolina Travel Department advertisement*

Texas does not, like any other region, simply have
indigenous dishes. It proclaims them. It congratulates you,
on your arrival, at having escaped from the slop pails of the
other forty-nine states.

> *Alistair Cooke*

I worry about dessert with a greater specific gravity than the nickel-iron core of the planet.

Jack Butler, on fruitcake

When I was a child and the snow fell, my mother always rushed to the kitchen and made snow ice cream and divinity fudge—egg whites, sugar and pecans, mostly. It was a lark then and I always associate divinity fudge with snowstorms.

Eudora Welty

It's like broiled crow with tobacco dressing. I can eat it, but I don't hanker for it.

Duncan Hines, referring to pot likker

The true Southern watermelon is . . . chief of this world's luxuries, king by the grace of God over all the fruits of the earth. When one has tasted it, he knows what the angels eat.

Mark Twain

241
EATING
AND
DRINKING
IN
THE
SOUTH

Who but a god could have come up with the divine fact of okra?

James Dickey

One of life's most delightful elixirs, which studies prove will heal the sick and occasionally raise the dead.

Lewis Grizzard, on Coca-Cola

At a grocery store on [Manhattan's] Upper West Side called Gourmet Garage, I came upon a tray full of cold Krispy Kreme doughnuts for sale beneath a sign that read, "Fresh from the Antebellum South."

"Well, now," I said to the man behind the counter. "They can't be any too fresh."

Roy Blount Jr.

"Too Much Pork for One Fork"

Title of a song by Southern Culture on the Skids

They fell in love with the memory of old Coke.

> *Roy Stout, director of market research for Coca-Cola, on the public's reaction to New Coke*

The Southern Kitchen

If you want world-class fried chicken, you need to find some that was cooked by a Baptist.

> *Ludlow Porch*

Cookbooks in the South outsell everything else but the Bible.

> *Julia Reed*

In the year I was born, 1960, non-farm households in the South spent two-and-a-half times the national average on cornmeal and twice the average on lard.

> *Julia Reed*

243
EATING
AND
DRINKING
IN
THE
SOUTH

I learned to cook from my grandmother. She was one of those cooks who couldn't tell you how to do something; she had to show you. She measured milk in a half of an egg shell. The chocolate cake recipe calls for butter the size of an egg and a dime's worth of salt. I've learned to do it her way if I want the recipe to work.

Darlene Slaymaker, owner of Yesterday's restaurant in Albany, Georgia

She'd fried up a huge mess of catfish that Grandpa and my father had caught that morning in the Sunflower River. There were homemade hushpuppies and a tangy slaw she'd made of shredded cabbage, chopped celery, sweet pickles, and mayonnaise, with a dab of French's mustard thrown in to enhance the flavor.

Steve Yarbrough

Eating Out

**You know I long for you. You melt in my mouth
I'm crazy about you, pretty golden hashbrowns.**

> *Billy Dee Cox, "Waffle House Hashbrowns (I Love You)"*

Let me tell you one thing. Joe can't eat no Popeyes fried
chicken. That would tear his stomach up from now till the
end of this week.

> *Onnie Lee Logan, on why she had to interrupt an interview
> to fix her husband's lunch*

WHEN YOU EAT, PAY ER RUN
CAUSE MR. BOSS GOT HES GUN

> *Sign outside a Vicksburg, Mississippi, restaurant, as recorded
> in Langston Hughes's* The Big Sea

245
EATING
AND
DRINKING
IN
THE
SOUTH

The South is anywhere below the line where restaurants will bring you grits in the morning (and the Deep South is where they bring the grits without asking).

Fred Powledge

Why do I accept the fast-food biscuits foisted upon me by the national chains? Shouldn't I, a Southerner born and bred, be sitting in a little café in the shadow of the Floyd County courthouse right about now, talking college sports over a platter of eggs, bacon, and scratch buttermilk biscuits baked by somebody's dear old grandmother?

John T. Edge

It is dazzling to discover smorgasbord at a South Carolina inn or a Caesar salad in Arkansas. Surely, we think, such internationalism is a good sign, rather like the Daughters of the American Revolution voting for an increase in foreign aid.

Eleanor Perenyi

They started a bunch of corporations.
Everybody got into speculation.
Chicken stock was so alarmin',
Nearly made Dow Jones go back to farmin'.

Billy Edd Wheeler, referring to the proliferation of restaurant chains owned by country music stars, in "Fried Chicken and a Country Tune"

~~~~

Tweet Yourself to a Twitty Burger.

Advertising slogan for Conway Twitty's chain of restaurants

~~~~

At Magnolias, Barbara Mandrell's newly opened temple of haute cuisine in Franklin, Tennessee, fried chicken has been replaced with free-range chicken "stuffed with crumbled sausage and cornbread atop a sauté of sweet yellow corn crowned by fried parsnips." The yuppie in the cowboy hat has arrived.

Mark Lane

EATING
AND
DRINKING
IN
THE
SOUTH

If you ask a Southerner to name the best meal he ever ate, he will invariably recall something that his mama or grandmamma . . . fixed at home. If you ask a Yankee . . . he will invariably name a four-star, impossible-to-get-into restaurant, and usually not even mention the actual food.

> *Julia Reed*

Food in Society

It means, "I love you. And I am sorry for what you are going through and I will share as much of your burden as I can." And maybe potato salad is a better way of saying it.

> *Will D. Campbell, on the tendency of Southerners to take food to families in mourning*

If we black folk can salvage something as unpalatable as the n-word, then surely we can reclaim the watermelon.

> *John Simpkins*

If you're going to reduce Southern Living, the whole enterprise and all of its success and everything about it to one word, it would be very easy: cornbread.

John Logue, former editor of Southern Living

You hear a lot of jazz about Soul Food. Take chitterlings: the ghetto blacks eat them from necessity while the black bourgeoise has turned it into a mocking slogan. . . . Now they have the price of a steak.

Eldridge Cleaver

The cult of Soul Food is a form of black self-awareness and, to a lesser degree, of white sympathy for the black drive to self-reliance. It is as if those who ate the beans and greens of necessity in the cabin doorways were brought into communion with those who, not having to, eat those foods voluntarily as a sacrament.

Gene Baro, in a 1970 Vogue *interview*

249
EATING
AND
DRINKING
IN
THE
SOUTH

Soul Food grew in the way that soul music grew—out of necessity, out of the need to express the "group soul."

Pearl Bowser

The Moonpie is more than a snack. It is a cultural artifact.

William Ferris

We were always given enough to eat, but we hated the lumpy milk and mushy eggs, and sometimes we'd stop off at the house of one of the poorer families to get some peanut butter and crackers.

Maya Angelou, on eating during the Depression

I don't believe LJ envied my lighter shade of skin, but it was obvious he coveted my access to a bologna sandwich on white, store-bought bread with mayonnaise.

Tim McLaurin

You can tell how long a couple has been married by whether they are on their first, second, or third bottle of Tabasco.

Bruce R. Bye

Southerners can't stand to eat alone. If we're going to cook a mess of greens we want to eat them with a mess of people.

Julia Reed

Booze

A man shouldn't fool with booze until he's 50; then he's a damn fool if he doesn't.

William Faulkner

In 1980 I moved back to South Carolina, where drinking oneself to death gracefully could more readily be passed off as a full-time job.

Blanche McCrary Boyd

251
EATING
AND
DRINKING
IN
THE
SOUTH

You're just a whiskey drinkin' woman,
We never will get very far,
Because every time I wanna find you
I just go around some whiskey bar.

> *Memphis Slim, "Whiskey Store Blues"*

I know folks all have a tizzy about it, but I like a little bourbon of an evening. It helps me sleep. I don't much care what they say about it.

> *Lillian Carter, on attitudes toward drinking in Plains, Georgia*

I *had* to drink. That's where I got the courage to get in front of those drunks in the honky-tonks. If I hadn't been drinking with them, I'd a got scared and run home.

> *Carl Perkins*

Most of them around here, they're pretty good country people until they start drinking.

> *Buford Trotman, retired pastor of the Sand Mountain Holiness Church, on the citizens of Henagar, Georgia*

Oh don't you be like me,
Oh don't you be like me,
Drink your good sweet cherry wine
And let that whiskey be.

Leadbelly, "Alabama Bound"

"What's the Use of Getting Sober?"

Title of a Louis Jordan song

The grand old drink of the South originated on the banks of the Mississippi in New Orleans, Louisiana, U.S.A.

The label on a bottle of Southern Comfort

Don't try me nobody,
cause you will never win.
Don't try me nobody,
cause you will never win.
I'll fight the Army and Navy.
Somebody gives me my gin.

"Gin House Blues"

253

EATING
AND
DRINKING
IN
THE
SOUTH

I got drunk one night. Actually several nights in a row and it scared me. When I came to, I believed I had been on a "running drunk" for two days. It was the first time that had ever happened to me, and I'd always said it never would. Now I had done it, and it hadn't seemed that hard.

Larry Brown, "92 Days"

Yes, anything to drive away the blues.

John Wilkes Booth, after being offered a drink when he heard that Lee surrendered at Appomattox

The only way that I could figure they could improve upon Coca-Cola . . . is to put rum or bourbon in it.

Lewis Grizzard, on Coca-Cola's announcement that it was changing its formula

Well, between Scotch and nothin', I suppose I'd take Scotch. It's the nearest thing to good moonshine I can find.

William Faulkner

One cannot create immortal literature when one is potted—Mr. Faulkner's work was too finely crafted, too profound, to be the work of a drunkard. . . . When he worked, he was sober. Alcohol was an escape for him.

Howard Bahr, curator of Rowan Oak from 1976 to 1993

The tools I need for my work are paper, tobacco, food, and a little whiskey.

William Faulkner

I'm not going to come down on booze, because it's done a great deal for me, frankly. It's like scolding an old friend now that you don't need him.

Barry Hannah

What you need for breakfast, they say in East Tennessee, is a jug of good corn liquor, a thick beefsteak, and a hound dog. Then you feed the beefsteak to the hound dog.

Charles Kuralt

255

EATING
AND
DRINKING
IN
THE
SOUTH

The nectar of the gods came from the vine
But what can compare with Georgia moonshine?

Alexander A. Lawrence, "Madeira and Moonshine"

[My father] shaved every morning at the water shelf on the back porch with a straight razor and always smelled of soap and whiskey. I knew mama did not like the whiskey, but to me it smelled sweet, better even than the soap.

Harry Crews

[Mississippians] will vote dry as long as they can stagger to the polls.

Will Rogers

My father would say that the only difference between Mississippi (when it was a dry state) and its neighbor Tennessee, which was wet, was that in Tennessee a man could not buy liquor on Sunday.

Willie Morris

The Southern Landscape

Let us begin by discussing the weather, for that has been the chief agency in making the South distinctive.

U.B. Phillips, Life and Labor in the Old South

Climate and Weather

If snow falls infrequently on the Southern land, the sun displays no such niggardly tendencies.

Clarence Cason

~~~

A townsman can never understand the significance of rain.

Andrew Lytle, from I'll Take My Stand

Now an' I'm goin' back down South,
Man, where the weather suits my clothes.
Now I done fooled around in Chicago,
Yeah, an' I got done almost froze.

Sonny Boy Williamson I, "Down South"

Can one imagine Faulkner writing *Absalom, Absalom!* under the spell of central air? One might, indeed, discover a direct relationship between the rise of air-conditioning and the decline of the creative fury of the Southern writer.

Fred Hobson

This is not a preserving climate. . . . This is a softening climate, a loosening, rotting climate. Every living being . . . and whatever is made of a living thing . . . is subject to its laws.

Pam Durban, referring to Charleston, South Carolina

Snow in the South is wonderful. It has a kind of magic and a mystery that it has nowhere else. And the reason for this is that it comes to people in the South not as the grim, unyielding tenant of Winter's keep, but as a strange and wild visitor from the secret North.

Thomas Wolfe

~~~~~

Everybody talks about the weather, but nobody does anything about it.

Southern proverb

~~~~~

Air conditioning cannot be a grand success in the South for the reason that the honest natives of the region recognize the natural summer heat as a welcome ally in that it makes the inside of houses and offices agreeably uninviting, if not actually prohibited territory.

Clarence Cason

It was hot as only a day can be hot in the middle of an airless field in Georgia.

Harry Crews

Tennessee summer days were not made for work; in fact, many a resident had doubted that they were made at all, but that they sprang to life from the cauldrons of hell.

Carl Rowan

It was hard to understand how people had made out here before air conditioning and screens.

V. S. Naipaul

Roy said that if a foreign power were to invade the country and kill thirty people, billions of dollars would be spent in retaliation and further defense. But when a tornado hits and kills thirty people, we say it's an act of God and go on. Now that's not right.

Hank Bass, tornado researcher at the University of Mississippi

I have seen storms in the Texas Panhandle, for example, where it's just as if God created it for you to see. The hail shafts, the rain shafts—all of it is visible and it speaks to you.

Roy Arnold, tornado researcher at the University of Mississippi

There had been no rain in almost two weeks, and when you stepped between the corn rows, the dust rose and hung, not falling or blowing in the windless day, but simply hanging interminably between the purple shucks of corn.

Harry Crews

On May 11, 1894 in Bovina, Mississippi, a gopher turtle measuring six by eight inches, entirely encased in ice, fell out of the sky along with the hail, and even my *Mississippi Almanac* lists it as the state's all-time "Most unusual weather occurrence."

Julia Reed

The sun went behind a cloud and the wind went up, and we were almost dark, in a sudden chilly breeze, a momentary violent change almost as if to another, Northern geography. In July, out of the heat, it seemed pure magic.

Barry Hannah

Take away the environment of the South and you might as well have New Jersey.

Fred Powledge

Flora and Fauna

Anyone who fancies homegrown, sun-ripened tomatoes (the only kind worth eating) is well acquainted with hornworms.

Janet Lembke

Anything you feed an emu in the morning, you will see again by that afternoon.

Emu farmer B. A. Teague, on the bird that is becoming one of the most popular small livestock investments in Mississippi

~~~~

Hey, hey, bo-weavil, don't sing them blues no more.
Bo-weavil's here, bo-weavil's everywhere you'll go.

Ma Rainey, "Hey Bo-Weavil"

~~~~

**The boll weevil was a little black bug,
Come from Mexico they say.
Come all the way to Georgia,
Just a-lookin' for a place to stay.**

"The Boll Weevil"

~~~~

A possum is just like a buzzard. It will eat anything that is dead. The longer dead the better.

Harry Crews

The worms had lots of legs and two little things on their heads that looked like horns. They were about an inch long, sometimes as long as two inches, and round and fat and made wonderful things to play with.

Harry Crews, describing cutworms

When I was a little bitty baby, my mama done rocked me in the cradle,
in them ole cotton fields back home.

"Ole Cotton Fields Back Home"

Cotton is king. . . . No power on earth dares make war upon it.

South Carolina senator James Hammond

I'd rather see a world tangled with kudzu than sodded with grass.

Vic Miller

Kudzu is the scourge of the Deep South, and if we didn't know differently, we'd swear it was a secret weapon that had been brought down from up yonder during the "War of Northern Aggression."

Mildred Jordan Brooks

Environment

What sets one Southern town apart from another, or from a Northern town or hamlet, or city high-rise? The answer must be the experience shared between the unknowing majority (it) and the knowing minority (you).

Maya Angelou

Daddy looked at the sun to see what time it was. He could come within five or ten minutes by the position of the sun. Most of the farmers I knew could.

Harry Crews

I had always been fascinated by the Southern roadside. When I was young, my family moved across the South from Tennessee to Texas, and I fell in love with Stuckey's—the salt and pepper shakers, the banners, and Southern doodads.

Charles Reagan Wilson

The wild Florida, the Florida of oil-less waters and sable night skies, of footprint-free beaches and fearless animals, is as much a construct of our will as the Florida of friendly mermaids, talking animals, waterskiing Aquamaids, and highly trained shrubbery.

Diane Roberts

Everybody likes to rhapsodize about how beautiful the rural life is. The rural life, as I knew and experienced in childhood, is, without exception, dreadful. It makes a man brutal to animals, to himself. It makes him callous and unfeeling.

Harry Crews

When it's darkness on the Delta,
That's the time my heart is light.
When it's darkness on the Delta,
Let me linger in the shelter of the night.

The Red Tops

A perfect climate above a fertile soil, yields to the
husbandman every products of the temperate zone. . . .
There, are mountains stored with exhaustless treasures;
forest, vast and primeval, and rivers that, tumbling or
loitering, run wanton to the sea.

Henry Grady

Southern Scenes

In Louisiana there are stretches of bayou country whose
beauty is of a nature such as only the Chinese poets have
captured.

Henry Miller

We fell silent to hear the water and the woods. Downstream below us two tall poplars stood on either side. The space between their branches was like a big window and while Johnson and I watched, a bird cut straight and quick through the space, gliding from one shadow to the other. But I couldn't say what kind of bird, dark against light.

Fred Chappell, I Am One of You Forever

I forgot my shirt at the water's edge.
The moon is low tonight.
Nightswimming deserves a quiet night.

R.E.M., "Nightswimming"

The banks of the river rose sharply, supreme in their late-September dry green, brown, nearly red, nearly yellow foliage. The banks then gave way to pastoral hills, the staring cows, a few circling scavengers and two or three abandoned tractors.

Linda Peal White, describing the White River in Arkansas

From underground, somewhere, salt water,
brackish at least, mineral salts, filled up the
swamp and broadened it far across the Delta.
The water seemed limitless, everywhere, even to
a boy who grew up on the island.

Lewis Nordan, Sharpshooter Blues

This is the South I knew as a child. Swamp and palmetto
and "sinks" and endless stretches of pines slashed and
dripping their richness into little tin cups that glint like
bright money. Twisting sand roads . . . warm soft sand that
you play in; quicksand in which you die.

Lillian Smith

From the exterior, the building appears nothing
more than the pressboard and tin remains of an
old country church. An oil-caked transmission
and a scattering of log stumps sit by the
entrance beneath a yellow lamp and the rotted,
white beams of the porch roof.

Jonathan Miles, describing Junior Kinbrough's juke joint

Have you ever seen the Blue Ridge Mountains, boy?
Or the Chattahoochee, or the honeysuckle blue?

Drivin' 'n' Cryin', "Honeysuckle Blue"

If there is a finer place than Charleston in the spring, when azaleas bloom in every garden behind every wrought-iron gate on every winding street, I don't know it.

Charles Kuralt

I had forgotten springtime in the South, the dogwoods and the azaleas and the girls in halter tops in the gallery on the sixteenth hole at Augusta National.

Lewis Grizzard

In Mississippi it is difficult to achieve a vista.

Barry Hannah, "Testimony of Pilot"

I saw it at night. It got dark and it was December and those lights came on and I said, "Gosh, I must be in heaven." Then a mosquito bit me and I knew I wasn't.

Joe Sampite, mayor of Natchitoches, Louisiana, on his first visit to the town

And the little bitty baby draws a nice clean breath
   from over his beaming mama's shoulder.
He's staring at the worldly wonders that stretch just as far
   as he can see,
But he'll stop staring when he's older.

Vic Chesnutt, "New Town"

It is a wonderful, almost magical lake. High bluffs wooded with oaks and hickories rise up over the east side, and the water is dark yet somehow invested with a strange clarity that often lets you see the fish when it strikes.

Larry Brown

Along the eastern edge of town, where the levee runs high and wide, the Arkansas River spreads out broad like a plain, with the cotton fields beyond it, at harvest time a shallow sea of widening white bolls, the air thick with the dust of cotton.

Lorian Hemmingway, describing Pine Bluff, Arkansas

Somewhere, at the edge of a field
Dusk has set on fire, a horse
Lifts its broad head from the grass
And, like some beautiful machine,
Makes its way toward the sound
Of a bell in the distance.

Joseph Bolton, "Twilight"

The Everchanging South

People look and see all the obvious signs of homogenization, but go to the Stop 'n' Shop in Connecticut and try to find some okra.

John Logue, former editor of Southern Living

The Obvious Signs of Homogenization

Now that Leroy has come home to stay, he notices how much the town has changed. Subdivisions are spreading across western Kentucky like an oil slick. . . . The farmers who used to gather around the courthouse square on Saturday afternoons to play checkers and spit tobacco juice have gone. It has been years since Leroy has thought about the farmers, and they have disappeared without his noticing it.

Bobbie Ann Mason, from Shiloh

It disturbed me to hear this news, in much the same way I'd be disturbed to hear about the opening of a Starbucks in my old neighborhood.

Alan Jacobs's reaction when his friend told him of a store devoted exclusively to fly fishing opening in Birmingham

You can go to any gathering of businessmen in Atlanta, and I'll bet you five dollars to a ginger cake that at least fifty percent of them will not be natives.

Edward D. Smith, chairman of First National Bank of Atlanta

There were two theaters in Oxford, The Lyric and The Ritz. They were both on Van Buren Avenue. One has become an office building and the other has become retirement apartments.

Oxford, Mississippi-native Milly Moorhead

Every time I look at Atlanta I see what a quarter of a million Confederate soldiers died to prevent.

John Shelton Reed

As far as historical sweep goes, the most influential Southern institutions today, I guess, are Wal-Mart, CNN, the forthcoming Atlanta Olympics, mostly soulless country music, and a feel-your-pain policy-wonk president.

Roy Blount Jr., in 1995

A poster child for sprawl.

Atlanta, according to Denise Wright of the Buckhead Area Transportation Management Association

The magisterial Mouse arrived and transformed the pretty, dull solar plexus of Florida—the counties of Polk and Lake, Orange and Osceola—into a ruthlessly planned and scripted "Magic Kingdom," where the palm trees are, more often than not, artificial.

Diane Roberts

Even the loneliest old ladies get social calls,
Where they dine and talk about their savior.
And the grass roots effort to incorporate
Elects a smiling mayor.

Vic Chesnutt, "New Town"

If I leave Mississippi . . . it will be because the pervasive
football culture bores me and the proliferating Kentucky
Fried Chicken stands appall me, and the neon lights have
begun to replace the trees.

Alice Walker

Air conditioning and television have taken us
inside to be passive voyeurs of a fake world
made in Hollywood and New York.

John Egerton

Like Coca-Cola, its principle benefactor, and like Atlanta
itself, Emory University aspires to be more international
than Southern.

Doug Cumming

The Agrarians vs. Corporate America

All tend to support a Southern way of life against what may be called the American or prevailing way; and all as much as agree that the best terms in which to represent the distinction are contained in the phrase, Agrarian *versus* Industrial.

> *From the introduction to* I'll Take My Stand: The South and the Agrarian Tradition

Those who labor in the earth are the chosen people of God.

> *Thomas Jefferson*

I'm glad my son doesn't have to toil in a tobacco field all day long, as I did, but I wonder if he's missing out on something.

> *Tim McLaurin*

"If I had Nesus, I could rule ne world. Wit Nesus, I'd be bigger nan Wal-Mart and IBM both together. I know in my heart nat Nesus Christ could write more orders nan all my other salesmen put together. Nat's one goddamn ning I know about Nesus Christ."

The Boss, in Harry Crews's The Mulching of America

We can accept the machine, but create our own attitude toward it.

Stark Young, from I'll Take My Stand: The South and the Agrarian Tradition

The South is no longer a conquered territory . . . but a protest, articulate and constructive, is needed against another conquest, a conquest of the spirit.

Herman Clarence Nixon, from I'll Take My Stand: The South and the Agrarian Tradition

The Agrarian South, therefore, whose culture was impoverished but not destroyed by the war and its aftermath, should dread industrialism like a pizen snake.

Andrew Lytle, from I'll Take My Stand: The South and the Agrarian Tradition

The twelve Southerners [in *I'll Take My Stand: The South and the Agrarian Tradition*] were correct, and virtually alone at the time, in their insistence upon the importance of the local.

Wendell Berry

The reduction of the farm population . . . has been a joint project of industrial liberals and industrial conservatives.

Wendell Berry

[Man] goes on, he continues, he has outlived the dinosaur, he has outlived the atom bomb, and I'm convinced in time he can even outlive the wheel.

William Faulkner

The South as a state of mind is expiring, and everybody is too busy building skyscrapers and making money to notice.

Dale Bumpers

It's strange that anti-corporate, anti-materialistic, pro-environment opinions are never described as conservative anymore.

Hal Crowther

[Industrialism] needs to be strongly governed or it will destroy the economy of the household.

John Crowe Ransom

In spite of its resistance to change and good advice . . . [no] section of the South has been spared the cultural and spiritual blight—the grim consequences of the mass-market society that [Robert Penn] Warren and his Fugitives blamed on the Yankee capitalists.

Hal Crowther

Old South, New South

The South has been notorious for mythologizing itself. That part of the mind of the South which does not know itself persistently wishes to see the Old South, before the war, as a kind of Eden.

James Applewhite

Perhaps that is the biggest difference between the Old South and the New South: black people, for the most part, have lost their fear of white people.

Valerie Boyd

The only difference between the Old South and the New South, my friend says, is the New South has McDonald's and Rastafarians.

Valerie Boyd

The South, one might say, is a tree with many age rings, with its limbs and trunk bent and twisted by all the winds of the years, but with its tap root in the Old South.

W. J. Cash

Before and since Henry Grady used the term in 1886, every generation of Americans has been told that the South of its day was a New South.

Edgar T. Thompson

My definition of a New South would be a South in which it never occurred to anybody to mention the New South.

Walker Percy

Once upon a Southern time,
On this great plantation,
Life was like a fairy tale
Filled with romance.

*"Once Upon a Southern Time," as performed at
Dolly Parton's Dixie Stampede*

Nostalgia is a mercy much like whiskey; it becomes a handicap when it intoxicates you and a curse when you can't sober up.

Hal Crowther

The South is full of stories... Now, there's a home for all of them.

–Turner South

TURNER SOUTH ®

Television, Southern Style

turnersouth.com